D0090279

Remember Who You Are

Remember Who You Are

Life Stories That
Inspire the Heart and Mind

☙ ☙ ☙

Daisy Wademan

In Collaboration with
Professors of Harvard Business School

Harvard Business School Press
Boston, Massachusetts

Cataloging In Publication Data is available
Library of Congress Control Number: 2004002150
ISBN 1-59139-284-5

The paper used in this publication meets the requirements
of the American National Standard for Permanence of Paper
for Publications and Documents in Libraries and Archives
Z39.48-1992.

"A Fall Before Rising: The Story of Jai Jaikumar (A)" and "A Fall Before
Rising: The Story of Jai Jaikumar (B)" (Harvard Business School Publishing cases 9-600-047 and 9-600-048, respectively) by Richard Squire,
Sarah Vickers-Willis, and Harry Wilson, prepared under the supervision
of Professor H. Kent Bowen. Copyright © 2000 by the President and
Fellows of Harvard College. Adapted with permission of the President
and Fellows of Harvard College and with permission of the authors.

"Ideas, Policies, and Outcomes in Business History" by Thomas McCraw.
Business and Economic History Second Series, Volume Nineteen (1990),
Copyright © 1990 by the Business History Conference. Excerpts adapted
with permission of the author and with permission of the Business History Conference.

"Katharine Hepburn and Me" Copyright © 2003 by Rosabeth Moss
Kanter. Reproduced with permission of Rosabeth Moss Kanter.

"The Stuffed Bird" by Jeffrey F. Rayport. Copyright © 2003 by Jeffrey F.
Rayport. Reproduced with permission of Jeffrey F. Rayport.

For Paul

Contents

MANAGING YOURSELF

LEADING OTHERS

BUILDING VALUES

Acknowledgments

If I were to sufficiently thank every single person who has helped me throughout the long and sometimes difficult process of writing this book, this acknowledgments section would take longer to read than the volume itself. However, the generous support of certain friends, mentors, and colleagues — not to mention the contributing professors — deserves special mention, and I would therefore like to offer them here a sincere and heartfelt "thank you."

Eighteen months ago, Nitin Nohria helped me to get the ball rolling on this project, immediately seeing merit in my raw idea and urging me to pursue it. Throughout the entire process, his tactical advice and doses of encouragement have been invaluable. While I am appreciative for all of his assistance and advice, I am particularly so for his introduction to the incomparable Helen Rees, my agent. Minutes into our first phone call, I knew it was going to be a joy to work with Helen, and over time that initial impression has proved true a thousand times over. With humor and good grace, Helen guided me through the daunting task of turning my one-page summary into a full-fledged proposal, and, over the past year, into a manuscript. Her talents have benefited this book enormously. Thanks are due also to Helen's colleague, Joan Mazmanian.

It has been both an honor and a pleasure to work with the talented staff of the Harvard Business School Press. As acquiring editor, Suzanne Rotondo spotted the potential for this book and put her support behind it; she also provided critical feedback on several early essay drafts. When Suzanne moved on, the extraordinary Hollis Heimbouch picked up the project without a hitch, and it has been my privilege to work with her since. With her unerring editorial eye, Hollis was instrumental in helping me shape each and every chapter; the themes, messages, and writing are inestimably better for her efforts. For her amazing energy, talent, and belief in this book, she has my humble thanks. I am also indebted to Carol Franco and Walter Kiechel for bringing this project on board; to Astrid Sandoval for her excellent editorial and structural suggestions and logistical oversight throughout the process; to Mike Fender, for a wonderful jacket design. Special thanks goes to the talented members of the marketing, publicity, and sales teams for their vigorous efforts on the book's behalf: Gayle Treadwell, Sharon Rice, Susan Minio, Leslie Zheutlin, Daisy Blackwell Hutton, Mark Bloomfield, Zeenat Potia, and Christine Turnier-Vallecillo.

As I labored to translate these stories and observations from spoken format onto the page, my job was made easier and my end product better by the hard work of three gifted people. Connie Hale's work as line editor dramatically increased the clarity and readability of this entire manuscript; she deftly sharpened key points while helping me make the language both more graceful and more vivid. (If there are muddy ideas or clunky sentences anywhere, the fault is mine, not Connie's.) Sebastian Stuart lent a hand in shaping several pieces, particularly when time got tight. Stephanie Murg transcribed interviews and checked facts at a dizzying speed and pored over essay drafts with a fresh set of reader's eyes, offering excellent suggestions for improvement.

While in preparing this volume I have consistently benefited from an awe-inspiring array of talents, my greatest honor has been working with professors of Harvard Business School. For sharing their stories and speeches, ideas and observations, I am deeply grateful to them. Over the past year each has given generously and unflaggingly to this project and gone out on a personal limb in having his or her stories and musings set down on paper. They have all done so despite their own busy schedules and pressing deadlines, and several in the face of extremely difficult personal circumstances. Their thoughts and words were the original inspiration for this book—and it is my fervent hope that this book, in return, is a fitting tribute to them. I also send thanks to the faculty assistants who worked with me throughout the process: Chris Albanese, Leah Coffin, Cheryl Daigle, Susan Deavor, Rowena Foss, Kathy Ivanciw, Joan McDonald, Sandra Nunley, Elizabeth Scheele, and Elizabeth Sampson. Special appreciation goes, too, to Jean Cunningham in the Dean's office.

Several people offered me enormous and unselfish help as I worked to research this book, and each one has my most sincere appreciation. The inclusion of Jai Jaikumar's story, "A Fall Before Rising," would never have been possible without the generosity and forethought of five individuals. Professor Kent Bowen alerted me to the story and provided me a copy of the case study from which it was adapted. Richard Squire, Sarah Vickers-Willis (now Sarah Harden), and Harry Wilson, the case authors, had the inspiration and talent to have captured Professor Jaikumar's story so completely and movingly on paper—and the magnanimity to allow me to use it. When I contacted Mini Jaikumar to ask if I might include her husband's story in this collection, her response was as gracious as it was supportive; I am deeply in her debt. On a separate note, I am grateful to Jeffrey F. Rayport for the preparation of his essay, "The Stuffed Bird." I also send my thanks to Harvard Business School Publishing and to the Business History Conference for permission to adapt previously copyrighted work.

Finally, on a personal level: From the beginning to the end of this long and sometimes arduous journey, I have been materially aided and cheered along by innumerable friends. The patience they have shown me has been astounding, and their optimism has been contagious; they have made this trip not only possible, but worthwhile. Richard and Dr. Jennifer Linder opened their home to me repeatedly, offering me a place to write and to be. Richard read multiple drafts of my book proposal and offered excellent feedback, and Jennifer offered unsolicited—and much-needed—support in the project's very early phase. Geoffrey and Sarita Skidmore provided me a place to stay during my time in California, and Isabel Wademan repeatedly let me use her apartment as office and as mailbox. Erika Mikkelsen and

Anne Toker both offered crucial advice and guidance in the intellectual property area, despite being swamped with other demands. Tony Deifell lent his savvy not only as a photographer but also as an artist, sharing reflections on the creative process. Leslie Perlow and John Travers both gave concrete advice drawn from their own experiences as authors; Julie Russell's contributions were, quite literally, a charm. As he has done since my very first day in the professional world, Seneca Mudd kept me in stitches about the "craziness" and "mess." My mother, Mary Wademan, provided encouragement at many points along the way.

For the past year and a half Paul Sternhell has given me his unflagging support. He has pored over drafts of the manuscript; served as my CIO; endured one nearly ruined vacation which I spent working; and talked me down from a ledge too many times to count. For his faith in me and in this project, he has my profound gratitude.

This book is dedicated to him.

Remember Who You Are

Introduction

I put the cap back on my pen and leaned forward in my seat, elbows pressed against the desktop, eager for what I knew came next.

It was the last day of my third term at Harvard Business School—and, to put it mildly, the past few months had not gone well. At age twenty-seven, I found myself in the first down economy I had ever really known. Searching for a job, I attended nearly every one of the company information sessions held on campus; the few recruiters who did show up gave cheerful presentations about the wonderful places where they worked, hurriedly adding that they were taking summer intern applications only, please. Returning to my old firm was not an option, either: Recently acquired, it was laying people off in droves.

As the semester had worn on, I grew increasingly conflicted. Deep down, I knew I was lucky, and was grateful for what I had: more time in school, a good education, a network of friends I loved. Yet at the same time I couldn't help but feel worried, and more than a little scared. Tired of wondering how, come graduation, I would pay down my six-figure student loan, I kept desperately wishing for someone to sit me down at the kitchen table, pour me a cup of coffee, and explain—kindly but firmly—that everything would be all right. I began to doubt myself and my own choices, wondering if business was right for me after all. To continue with my chosen career, I needed a job, of course, but equally important, I needed to have some of my faith in the possibilities of business leadership restored. I needed to be reenergized, and reinspired.

Which is why I was sitting on the edge of my chair, waiting for the professor to speak.

Like every final course session at the school, this one had been a departure from routine. Gone were the case-study discussion and the class's typical rhythm: twenty hands in the air for every question the professor posed, students' comments zinging back and forth, a gradual untangling of opinions as to what the case's main character should do. Today, the blackboards stayed blank as the professor recapped the main themes of the material and described the format of the final exam. Around him, a hundred of us jotted notes, then put down our papers, closed our laptops, and grew silent, for the class was not yet over. In those last few minutes as our teacher, he was going to tell us a story from his own life—and give us the best advice he knew.

It was a school tradition, and in my first two semesters at school I had listened to nearly a dozen such send-offs—surprised at first, then rapt. I heard about professors' personal challenges, successes, and mistakes; moments when they—like me—had felt overwhelmed, or profoundly confused. There were funny anecdotes, ruminations that reflected years of thought, and tales that left us all near tears. One professor confidently delivered his speech with the help of elaborate PowerPoint slides, leaning nonchalantly against the desk; another paced the room, shoulders hunched, clutching a sheet of notes written on yellow legal paper. Some seemed lost in reverie as they spoke, as if they, like us, were hearing the story for the first time; many spoke casually, throwing in humorous asides. All the talks were different—as wildly different as the personalities of the people who gave them. Yet at the same time, they were consistent: All addressed how to create a better life—a *good* life—as a leader.

Each one of these speeches had left me mulling over its message for days. When I heard my peers recounting them over lunch in the cafeteria and beers at the local pub, I knew they had been deeply affected by them as well. And as I sat in class that December day, waiting for the professor to begin, I wondered: If just one story had the capacity to recharge me, what might a dozen or more of the very best of them do—for me, or for anyone else? Suddenly, I had a tiny glimmer of an idea.

Someone, I thought, *should really write these things down.*

EVEN BEFORE my rain-soaked graduation, I set about the task. Eighteen months later, this book is the result. It contains fifteen unique life lessons from Harvard Business School faculty members, some of them my own professors, and all of them experts in leadership education.

While these essays were inspired by advice given to young M.B.A. students at a particular moment in their careers, they are applicable to anyone who wants to enhance his or her ability as a leader, or who seeks a mentor while coping with a challenging profession. (For whether you are facing your first day on the job or already sit in the corner office, your need to stay inspired remains the same.) And, while these stories focus heavily on leadership in the business world, they can help to motivate leaders anywhere—in hospitals or classrooms, companies or families.

THROUGHOUT that broiling summer, I approached professors one by one to propose my idea. I chose stories that had particularly inspired me or that had had great impact on my classmates, adding the contributions of a few faculty members whom, quite simply, I admired, and whose thoughts and advice fit in with the spirit of this book. Rather than recording and transcribing their final addresses, I performed personal interviews, then worked closely with each professor to "translate" his or her thoughts and themes from the spoken word to the page. One, an ex-journalist, prepared his own from start to finish; for another, I adapted material prepared by three of his former students.

As I began to watch this manuscript take shape, I noticed that the themes of each essay—all centered around ideas of personal leadership—tended to interlock and overlap, yet, as complex human stories, they defied classification. But as I continued to work, I began to mentally sift them into four discrete categories, and I have organized the book according to these groups.

In "Gaining Perspective," professors address ways to think of yourself in the world. Jai Jaikumar explains what luck really is, and why you should "enjoy and celebrate your life." Through humorous anecdote,

[5]

Jeffrey Rayport helps you find confidence in moments of confusion and doubt. Richard Tedlow examines what it truly means to "be yourself" on the job; and Thomas McCraw suggests that before looking to your future, you must understand your past.

"Managing Yourself" provides techniques and tools—both tactical and psychological—for approaching your career. Steve Kaufman shines light on the pitfalls of moving up the ladder, while David Bell teaches how to take risks without fear. Nancy Koehn lets you get a glimpse of the complete, imperfect you, and Rosabeth Moss Kanter tells how a Hollywood legend helped her speak loud and clear.

In "Leading Others," each contributor explores how to motivate, inspire, and understand the people you work with. Kent Bowen provides a poignant reminder that the professional is always personal; and Frances Frei argues that being generous means being demanding—whether on the court or in the workplace. Tim Butler tells how to bring your employees' passions and talents to bear on the bottom line; and Tom DeLong shows how to have positive impact on those around you everywhere, and every day.

Three professors explore what it means to do good and do well in "Building Values"—and why business and conscience do mix. Hank Reiling demonstrates what race cars have to do with leadership; and Nitin

Nohria suggests a unique way to preserve a cherished legacy. Finally, Kim Clark offers motivation for the road ahead as he encourages you to "remember who you are."

AS YOU READ each chapter, you will hear an utterly distinct voice. Each professor tells a story with a personality, background, message, and style different from the rest. Some of these voices will grab your attention, speaking directly to your current situation or past experience. Others may make points you disagree with, or dwell on an aspect of leadership that comes easily to you. Many of the lessons will be brand-new; others you may have learned long ago but forgot along the way.

I hope you will find that the whole of this collection is greater than the sum of its parts, and that as you listen to these disparate voices, they will draw you into dialogue with yourself about what it means for *you* to be a leader. And I hope that they inspire you as they did me.

GAINING
PERSPECTIVE

A Fall Before Rising

Jai Jaikumar

RAMCHANDRAN ("JAI") JAIKUMAR, an expert in manufacturing sciences, won widespread recognition in 1976
with the development of the world's first multiplant, on-
line production control and distribution system. He received his undergraduate education at the Indian Institute of Technology and held advanced degrees from the
University of Oklahoma in engineering and the University of Pennsylvania's Wharton School of Business in decision sciences. He joined the business school faculty in
1980. While at Harvard, he developed close relationships
with his M.B.A. students, who took comfort from the
serenity he brought to the classroom.

An accomplished mountaineer, he died of natural
causes in Ecuador in 1998 while pursuing his "true vocation." He was fifty-three years old.

I'VE ALWAYS LOVED to mountain climb. As a boy
growing up in my native India, I would often
travel from my home in Madras and head north to
indulge my passion. By the time I was in college, I
spent nearly four months a year pursuing what I
called my "true vocation," biding the other eight, my
"spare time," as an engineer. As I grew increasingly
skilled at mountaineering, I became tempted by the
Himalayas, the world's tallest range, which forms
the border of the subcontinent.

In those mountains, more than thirty years ago, I
had an experience which both threatened and
changed my life, shaping my outlook on the relationship between privilege and responsibility, and
bringing me to a new passion altogether.

IT WAS A SUMMER day in 1966, and I stood with one
of my closest climbing buddies at the summit of a
Himalayan mountain, 24,000 feet above sea level.

At four in the afternoon, the light was already fading on the peaks, and there was little time left to enjoy the view.

Our final ascent had begun at high camp at two that morning. It had proved much rougher than the two of us had anticipated. We had originally set 1 P.M. as our turnaround time, when we would abandon the climb in order to make it safely back down to camp for the night. But when one o'clock came, the prospect of waiting a few more days to again challenge the summit held little appeal. Both of us were healthy, experienced climbers, and we decided to press on.

Our perseverance rewarded, we gazed out from the pinnacle—well aware that time was against us. After a short celebration, we began the descent. In the failing light we felt our way, gingerly tapping our ice picks to test the surface below as we inched downward.

The descent followed a particularly precarious ridge, where the wind had created a cornice—a slab of ice and snow that extends at certain points out beyond the solid rock. Climbers can't see the underlying structure of the cornice, can't tell how far it protrudes from the surface beneath, or how much weight it will hold. Recognizing the danger, my friend and I untied the ropes that bound us. Now, if one of us fell, he would not drag the other to his death.

I was in the lead. About to take my next step, I heard a loud, explosive sound. Instinctively, I jumped to one side and my friend jumped to the other as the cornice fractured and fell beneath us.

I landed on a sheer slope and for a split second was relieved to feel solid ground—but the terrain was so steep my feet slipped out from under me and I fell onto my back. I began to slide downward, within moments picking up tremendous speed, skidding nearly sixty miles an hour down the mountain's sharp pitch.

Having trained with experts, I knew the protocol in a crisis. Plunging down the mountain face, I rid myself of unnecessary gear so that any sharp objects—like my ice ax—wouldn't puncture my body. Somehow, miraculously, I remained conscious and managed to shed layer after layer, including my backpack full of provisions.

But I couldn't control my speed. The mounds of snow I hoped might slow my run did nothing— I merely punched through one after another. To guide my course, I dug my feet hard into the surface of snow and ice, hoping to avoid a fatal collision with the boulders that raced up at me from below. The friction from my slide against the abrasive surface of the mountain seared my clothes and lacerated my body.

Finally, the terrain leveled off and I skidded to a stop. I had lost more than 3,000 feet in altitude, tumbling more than a mile and a half down the slope. As I lay, semiconscious, I knew that my climbing suit, the only thing protecting me from the elements, had torn through. My skin was bloody and singed and much of my torso stripped raw, but the pain was dulled by shock and the fog of concussion. Aware that exposure to the extreme night cold would soon leave me immobile, I slowly drew myself to my feet.

It was agony. Using my legs to try to slow my rapid descent had severely damaged them, and the pain in my hip joints and in my feet was extreme. I looked around. None of the equipment I had shed during the descent had followed me to the same spot. Other than a small pack of food, I had lost all my supplies. Worse, my friend was nowhere in sight. Before making the climb I had scrutinized maps of the area, and intuition told me I had slid down the wrong face; our camp was on one side of the mountain, and I was on the other. Given my pain and the steep angle of the terrain, retracing my steps would be impossible.

Unless I could get farther down and find shelter before I passed out, I knew my chances for survival were slim. With no idea where I was or how far from civilization, I decided to walk—until I could walk no longer.

That descent would have been challenging even with no injuries and the proper gear. What would have taken six hours under normal conditions took me twenty-four. When I had to rest, I stopped and stood still or leaned against a large rock, knowing that if I sat down I might never get back to my feet. I walked day and night.

I can hardly describe those hours: the terrible loneliness and despair, the agonizing physical pain and cold—and the haunting knowledge that my friend had almost certainly perished.

Suddenly, I heard a dog barking in the distance. My spirits surged—human life was somewhere ahead! Struggling forward, I soon came on a small valley, heard faint voices and the sound of children laughing. (That laughter, I am certain to this day, was one of the sweetest sounds a person could ever hear.) I kept moving and reached a clearing with a small hut standing modestly at its center.

Overcome with relief and exhaustion, I collapsed.

I awoke to find a small woman, maybe forty years old, offering me food and water, cleaning my abrasions, and speaking in a language I could not understand. She must have come out of her hut to investigate the noise I made as I fell to the ground, and found me lying a few feet away: a foreign man, unconscious, body covered in ragged clothes, worn boots, and spots of dried blood. I tried to stand, but

[16]

my feet had become too swollen and my hips too weak to hold my weight.

For hours I lay motionless, unable to do anything but accept the food and water the woman offered me and to try to communicate through sign language that I needed to continue—to reach the camp on the opposite face of the mountain. It was clear to both of us that I could not travel in my current state. The pain had become so severe I could not even crawl.

To my amazement, the woman signaled that she intended to *carry* me down the mountain to the next village. Lifting me onto her back, she hauled me from the hut, walked five hundred feet or so, and then placed me down so she could rest. She drank some water, forced me to sip a bit, then lifted me onto her back again. We continued in this way, a few hundred feet at a time, for three whole days.

When we reached the next village the woman found the local officials, engaging them in an animated argument until they reluctantly agreed to transport me, on the back of a donkey, to a larger village with a hospital. The woman refused to leave me until my safe passage was assured, and refused to accept any payment for her kindness and generosity. She seemed satisfied with the knowledge that I would be safe. She simply gestured farewell, and departed.

From that village, I rode the donkey for two days (a much more painful trip, I might add, than the one on the back of the shepherd woman). During that time I began to take a broader perspective on the whole situation.

How fragile, I realized, my life was, and how drastically my personal circumstances could change in an instant. I pondered the source of the generosity of the shepherd woman, with whom I could not even carry on a conversation, yet who had given so much to me, unconditionally.

With these thoughts heavy in my heart, we finally arrived at the hospital, where I was delivered into the arms of an astonished physician. He quickly diagnosed a broken hip and fallen arches on both feet. My injuries were very serious, but would not be permanent.

My climbing companion had not been as fortunate. Confirming my worst suspicions, I learned that my friend remained missing, and was presumed dead.

MY PHYSICAL RECOVERY was rapid, but I could not stop thinking about my fall and the events in its immediate aftermath. Delivered from a moment of terrific hardship by pure chance, I was forced to consider the tremendous role that luck had long played for me both on and off that mountain. During my recuperation, I began to reflect on how fortunate I had been: lucky to have jumped to the right side of the cornice and survived, lucky to have walked in the right direction after my slide, lucky to have stumbled upon the hut and its magnanimous occupant, and lucky to recover as well as I did. Yet my good fortune was not limited to the weeks surrounding my fall; it extended instead back to the very earliest parts of my life: to my childhood, to the family who raised me, and to the education I had been privileged to receive. I realized that whatever success I had was born in my good fortune, and obligation was born in my own success.

Within a year of my mountain fall, constantly conscious of my gratitude to the shepherd woman, I planned my return to her village, hoping to somehow repay my enormous debt. Money, I knew, was of little use to her, but as I remembered the isolation of the area and the limited resources of its inhabitants, I had an idea. Why not try to improve the "luck" of the villagers by building a school and giving local children their first opportunity for an education? Over the next several months I raised funds to pay teachers' salaries and meet the costs of construction.

My idea to build that single school gradually grew into a mission. In the thirty years since my fall, I immigrated to the United States, earned my graduate degree, launched a career in manufacturing sciences, and became a full-time professor. Yet throughout that time, I have continued to raise money to support the construction and operation of schools in remote communities. All, of course, while continuing to pursue my true vocation, climbing mountain after mountain.

WHILE MY PASSION for climbing led me to scale that one particular peak, my fall helped me reach much greater heights, shaping my outlook on the world, and leading me to the advice that I give to all of my students, and that I want to share with you.

Relax.

The combined demands of career and family can be very stressful, I know. But no matter where you are personally or in your work, remember to relax— enjoy and celebrate your life.

Try to recognize your own advantaged position in the world, the "luck" given to you by a dedicated teacher or a loving parent. Above all, appreciate the responsibilities created when good fortune chose to smile upon you so abundantly.

Success is born in good fortune, and obligation is born in success. In creating luck for others, you yourself may reach the highest peak.

The Stuffed Bird

Jeffrey F. Rayport

JEFFREY RAYPORT taught at Harvard Business School for nine years. In 1999, he took a leave of absence from the school to establish and serve as chief executive officer of Marketspace LLC, a unit of the Monitor Group, a leading global consulting firm. Marketspace provides strategic advice, executive development, and software-based business intelligence to firms competing in the networked economy. Before becoming a professor, he worked in financial services and consulting, was a writer for *Fortune* magazine, and earned a Ph.D. from Harvard.

The e-commerce course he taught at the school was an elective, but routinely enrolled half the second-year class. He won the student-voted "Outstanding Professor" award a record three years in a row.

BEGINNING in the early 1990s, I taught a second-year elective course called Managing Market-space Businesses, which earned the distinction of being the first M.B.A. e-commerce course in the nation. Like all things Internet, the course started small, populated by a few true believers in the power of technology in business; it grew rapidly as mainstream business students aspired not to *Fortune* 500 corporate jobs but to their own (or others') entrepreneurial dreams.

The mania of dot-com ventures is now where it should be—an important, if short-lived, development in the history of business. The Internet did not "literally change everything," as it was fashionable to say only a few years ago. But at the time, there were plenty of big new ideas to consider (some with staying power and some without), and there were even more unanswered questions: What was the impact on business of a nearly ubiquitous global network that could conceivably connect everyone on earth?

How might networked businesses evolve to serve companies and customers in more efficient and effective ways? After graduation, how might our M.B.A. students advance new ideas in business when so many fundamental questions about the new economy, and its implications for managers, remained unanswered? It was, at the time, a kind of terra incognita.

There was little to go on other than the expectation that business would, in the future, be radically different from business in the past. At the same time, there was scant reliable evidence from which to draw many rigorous conclusions. Internet-related opportunities seemed to shift from one *Business Week* cover story to the next; an array of dazzling technologies relevant to business were evolving rapidly before our eyes; a frothy stock market induced staid corporations and equity firms to fund practically any venture that included buzzwords of the moment in their PowerPoint slide decks. It all added up to more promise of more opportunity—and with greater potential rewards—than any generation of young business leaders had ever seen.

But there was a dark side. As captivating as technology, interactive media, and networks were to some, especially by the late 1990s there was an increasing undertone in the air of greed and cynicism.

Greed because the rewards were so munificent (for some), cynicism because the pace at which business models went in and out of style implied the lack of an intellectual or moral core to this "revolution." To some, the "bubble" appeared a mass delusion, a vivid illustration of the madness of crowds. To others, it was a con game driven by the basest of business instincts and destined to end in terrible ways.

To seize this moment of opportunity and do something real required courage—courage to rise above the noise and the mania, courage to invent new models for business, as enabled by technology, that would create lasting value. Doing so would demand individual fortitude and integrity, self-confidence and an internal compass, and an authentic desire to make a difference—a positive difference—in the world. It would challenge anyone who sought such opportunities to make decisions under conditions of profound, even extreme, uncertainty.

In this sense, the challenges of launching a business or a career in the Internet era were entirely consistent with those of starting a career at any point in history—only more so. The pace of change today is arguably even more frenzied than it was five years ago, and the world is even more chaotic and confusing. Certainty in decision making, if it ever existed, is but a pipe dream today.

Thinking about these challenges, I am often reminded of an experience I had taking a final exam as an undergraduate at Harvard College, which, with a degree of poetic license, I will share by way of analogy.

IN THE SECOND SEMESTER of my sophomore year, against my better instincts, I enrolled in a zoology course. Why I took such a course, I do not know, since I had no particular interest in the field, beyond a long-standing admiration for lemurs, with their opposable thumbs and ringed tails, and a few other primate animals. I surely knew that I was planning to do little or nothing in life sciences in my career, interesting as the field was, so I can only chalk up this course selection to the recklessness of youth and the distribution requirements in force at the time. Be that as it may, here I was studying the genus and species of all manner of wild creatures and learning from wild-eyed graduate students what it meant to devote your career to the study of life forms, fossils, and other animal remains.

When it came time to take the final exam in the course, the format was somewhat odd. We were marched into what was then the college's largest exam-writing venue, the refectory in Memorial Hall (now a dining facility for freshmen). It's a grand wood-paneled room, part of a brick-and-stone, cathedral-like building constructed to honor the school's Civil War dead. On one end is an amphitheater that seats more than a thousand people. At the other end is a football field–sized hall that easily seats half that many at tables arrayed from wall to wall for its entire length. Back then, this was far from a gemütlich space. Other than the occasional alumni dinner, it was used for only two activities: to welcome scared, socially challenged freshmen to campus for the first time with a mind-numbing array of extracurricular activities on offer; and to administer exams.

When I think of exams I took in Memorial Hall, the phrase "economies of scale" comes to mind. The college would pack as many students from as many different courses as possible into that vast space and administer four-hour written exams en masse. (In those days, we wrote our exams in "blue books," since personal computers were still the size of small refrigerators and not widely used.) The person charged with giving the exam was an enormously corpulent man known only as "Doctor Proctor." The rumor was that Doctor Proctor was a graduate student of long standing—a "G-17," in the vernacular, which meant he had enrolled in a doctoral program seventeen years earlier and still not completed a dissertation. Such individuals seem to haunt research universities such as Harvard, and they tend, perhaps understandably, to feel somewhat bitter about their lots in life. In consequence, the typical Harvard undergraduate, much advantaged and with a bright future ahead, failed to qualify as a vision of joy to Doctor Proctor, who needed no provocation to express his sadistic tendencies. Many of us believed that Doctor Proctor gave exams year after year because he enjoyed doing so, especially given the chance to torture so many fine students under nearly medieval conditions.

And when I say medieval, I mean it. In my freshman year, I took a series of exams in Memorial Hall when a vast snowstorm blanketed Cambridge over a period of several days. Despite the arctic conditions outside, there was no heat in the hall. And despite the frigid temperatures inside the hall, Doctor Proctor sweated copiously and profusely. To overcome his own personal heat wave, Doctor Proctor would throw open the doors of the hall to embrace the great outdoors. In the midst of this storm, snow would waft in. I still recall scribbling a long essay on the Romantic poets under a bitterly cold wind, as snow swirled and fell on my blue book pages and the ink ran. Requests and complaints from desperate students failed to induce Doctor Proctor to close the doors; indeed, they aroused in him nothing more than a sneer of disgust.

Doctor Proctor kept his distance from the teeming masses, maintaining his aura of power by starting and stopping the exams using a deafening sound system that would have made Mussolini proud. He spoke into what looked like an original radio microphone from the 1930s, which he would grasp atop a tall chrome-metal stand. Of course, he used the same PA system to provide "helpful" time checks as exams progressed; these became so frequent (and loud) that they would inspire literal cries of distress from his charges. When Doctor Proctor was not using his sound system, he would sit at a desk at one end of the room, staring malevolently around him and drinking thirstily from half-gallon plastic bottles of RC Cola stored at room temperature behind his chair.

Taking a zoology exam in such an environment was especially odd, since the course only had two dozen students. We occupied just two short tables in the great expanse of the room. When the exam was about to begin, with Doctor Proctor preparing to bark his first set of orders into the microphone, our graduate assistant, with his usual haunted and di-sheveled look, strode through a side door with a lab-oratory cart transporting what appeared to be a large stuffed bird. I say "appeared" because the bird, which was standing upright, was covered in a burlap bag from its head almost to the ends of its feathers. Our graduate student, surely a soul mate of Doctor Proctor's, brought the cart to the end of our table and announced diffidently, "This is your final exam." As we cried out in perplexity and distress bordering on hysteria, he stated that in our exam we should put our semester's knowledge to use by characterizing the specimen of the bird as expertly as we could, inferring from the evidence before us its migratory patterns, its daily diet, its mating habits, its communications protocols, its flocking instincts, and, if possible, its genus and species. The exam would take the usual four hours, and we were allowed to examine the specimen closely, but with one important condition: We could not remove the burlap bag.

This was most unusual. To demonstrate a semester's worth of learning, we had nothing to go on but the paltry view of two spindly legs, a pair of claws mounted on a stand, and an inch or so of feathers hanging below the edge of the bag. Of course, it was possible to gauge the approximate mass and shape of the bird, but this was hardly comforting, given that we had to devise four hours' worth of written commentary regarding this unidentified, and seemingly unidenti-fiable, creature. Despite our dismay, however, we all stalwartly began our examination of the bird.

An hour or so into the exam, when most of us were furiously writing up our observations and con-clusions (as it were), one member of our class simply erupted. Since he was a short-fused individual gen-erally, I don't know why it took him an hour to react. But suddenly he jumped from his chair, charged over to the graduate assistant who was supervising us, and declared, "This exam is outrageous! This is an insult! I'm not doing this!" The graduate student, who had little in the way of gifts for interpersonal in-teraction, looked at him in a state of perplexity. Our classmate went on with his bellowing, holding forth about how many hundreds of specimens we had ex-amined over the course of the semester, how many hours we had spent in the dusty laboratories doing our course work, how much money this course had cost his parents in tuition bills, and so forth. Without question, he was fit to be tied. Several times Doctor Proctor used his microphone from across the room at debilitating decibel levels to order an end to this disruption, while our graduate student stood his ground with surprising tenacity. He calmly stated, "This is your final exam. Do it!"

It was only when this altercation reached a crescendo that I became aware that no one in the hall would write another word until the situation was resolved, since we were all observing this interchange with rapt attention. It was also clear that our classmate would not back down. Instead, he announced that for him, the exam was over; that he was submitting nothing; and that he would sue the college if he received a bad grade. He had better things to do with his time, he said.

The graduate student and Doctor Proctor, who with great labor had now approached the scene, confronted him and even ordered him to sit down. He refused. They demanded that he sit down. He began putting on his jacket and prepared to leave. They yelled at him to sit down, and he turned on his heel and headed toward the door.

The graduate student, whose face had become bright red with outrage, yelled across the hall, "Who do you think you are pulling a stunt like this?"

In response our classmate turned on him wildly, held up one foot in the air, pulled up his trousers to just below the knee—as if to reveal as much of himself to the graduate student as had been revealed to us of the bird—and yelled back, "I don't know! You tell me!"

And then he left.

It was hard for the rest of us to determine what was more bizarre—this interchange and its dramatic denouement or the format of our final exam. In any event, after watching our classmate storm out, we hapless would-be zoologists, dazed and bewildered, turned back to our blue books and finished writing our exams.

AS LIGHTHEARTED and perhaps literally sophomoric as this story may be, it was intended to convey an utterly serious message.

There are no certainties in life or business. There are no guarantees about outcomes. We make decisions—often critical and high-stakes decisions—often with inadequate data or data of the wrong kind. And the world is full of noise that's cause for distraction from the task at hand.

Charting the course of a business or a career under conditions of extreme uncertainty and accelerating change—which is increasingly the case for all of us in business—is not unlike writing an exam about a stuffed bird you can't actually see. You have little information to rely on except your own prior learning, experience, and instinct. The impediments to seeing your way are many: chaos in the world, irrational behavior of those around you, and an environment that can be cold and unforgiving. The key to moving forward is to realize that any kind of worthy goal—such as filling the pages of the blue book, finishing the exam, and completing the course—is to accept that available information is, and always will be, limited, and that great actions always require real, if educated, leaps of faith. Creative acts in business, as in life, demand courage and confidence. It's often easier to find reasons not to do new things, not to make decisions, not to take action. It's always easier to storm out of the room or settle for the status quo. To make a difference requires confidence in your own intelligence and abilities—and, as importantly, in the internal compass that tells you what's right in entrepreneurial and economic as well as moral and ethical terms.

As you move forward in your career, you will face many situations offering great promise and opportunity with little certainty about how best to proceed. As with the exam and the stuffed bird—where we had only two scrawny legs and a few visible feathers to go on—you will often have to make judgments and reach conclusions with little hard data at your disposal. When that happens, you will need courage and faith—faith in your own talents, faith in the talents of your business partners, faith in the potential for innovation, and faith in the possibilities for the world.

My strong admonition to you is simple. *Have such faith in yourself.* Don't squander the moments of great opportunity for fear of making the wrong decision. Don't miss the chances to make a difference in the world because of the comfort of inaction. Ignore the noise and turn off the hype. Have the courage to forge ahead. Listen to your passions. Consult your own internal compass. Think about yourself and about the human condition. And then do something truly great.

Be *Like* Yourself

Richard S. Tedlow

With his B.A. from Yale and doctorate in history from Columbia, RICHARD TEDLOW came to Harvard Business School on a research fellowship in 1978 and joined the faculty the following year as a professor of first-year marketing. Throughout his career, he has been deeply involved in the school's business history program. He is the author of *Giants of Enterprise: Seven Business Innovators and the Empires They Built,* named a top-ten business book of 2001 by *BusinessWeek* magazine.

He is so well known for his dry and self-deprecating wit in the classroom that the student newspaper has published a list of his humorous quips. "I am very good at predicting the past. I am *always* right," he deadpans to his business history classes. "Some of your other professors who deal with the future will frequently be wrong."

❦ ❦ ❦

When I began teaching at Harvard Business School, we junior faculty members — young and just starting out in our careers — would frequently watch experienced professors in action. We carefully observed each one's teaching style, which we evaluated by asking two questions.

First, did he (in those days the faculty was almost entirely male) ask the class specific questions and expect concise answers? Or were his queries vague, and did he let his students — to use the metaphor in vogue at the time — wander around, grazing in pastures?

Second, how self-revealing was he? You could sit through an entire semester with certain professors and learn next to nothing about them. Others *used* themselves to a much greater degree, really bringing their personalities, quirks, and senses of humor into the class.

Still developing my own professorial style, I was somewhat torn on that second point. I wanted to disclose enough of myself as a person to be an engaging teacher, but I was reluctant to put my life on display before rooms full of students who were essentially strangers. I wanted to strike a balance—to hit the right point on that continuum.

While still young and acutely untenured, I happened—by some wild miscalculation—to allow myself to be seated at lunch next to the late Anthony Athos, a renowned professor who held one of the school's endowed chairs. Tony's skill in the classroom was so great that he had been featured in a *Time* magazine cover story on "Great Teachers" only two years after finishing his doctorate. The two of us got to talking about the challenges of our profession. It was hard, I told him: On top of being an effective instructor, you have got to be yourself.

"No," he said. "You don't need to *be* yourself— but you've got to be *like* yourself."

I HAVE NEVER FORGOTTEN that advice, and over time I have come to understand better what it means: We can draw a nuanced distinction between our personal selves and our work selves—between who we are and what we do.

Drawing that separation is critical, but it is something that many businesspeople ignore, or misunderstand. It is not the same thing as the "work-life balance" so often discussed in the corporate world. That refers to the legitimate need to get out of the office and spend time on personal activities, to have enriching experiences outside one's job, and to keep from becoming alienated from family and friends.

But what Tony was driving at was something different. He was not talking about balancing *time*, but rather about balancing *identity*. Can you create and maintain a distinction between who you are at the office and who you are at home? And do you want to?

To my mind, the answer to both questions is "yes." That separation in identity provides you with significant advantages—not the least of which is privacy. As a professor, you teach a hundred or more students at a time. These are not people you know, and you do not want to feel as if you are putting your whole self on display for them, or handing out copies of your autobiography. So when you walk into class in the morning, it is helpful to have a *persona*—one very much *like* who you are. That persona is authentic; in cultivating it, you are not being a phony. But at the same time it is not really you: It is a different, professional version.

In effect, you can put a screen between your professional and personal lives: a porous boundary that allows commerce between the two while still marking the distinction. That screen allows the two areas of your life to remain separate without becoming exclusive, or binary—you do not need to move in and out of your work persona by flipping an on-off switch. Instead, the screen's permeability lets your "true" self flow into your work self as you desire and as circumstances permit. At the beginning of a term as a professor, for example, facing students you have never met, that persona must take center stage. Yet over the course of the semester, as you develop a greater connection to the class, the persona gives way to the personal. That screen provides privacy to the right degree, when needed. But it also offers other essential benefits—and not just in teaching, but in *any* job.

Developing a persona that is "like you" helps you withstand the slings and arrows you are bound to encounter during your career, and to survive while minimizing injury to your inner self. The working world is hard, and often beyond your power to control. As my father, who was in business for forty-five years, put it: It is cold out there. There are a lot of little murders in the professional arena, and especially if you are ambitious, you are going to take a lot of hits. Unpleasant things happen, particularly in tough times. Things go bad, companies go bankrupt, Lucent lays off ten thousand people. If you bring your entire identity into the workplace, you expose it to the assaults found in that environment. By thinking of your professional life as distinct from your home life, you can protect that interior space; you can maintain a "you" in there that is sheltered from the external forces acting upon you at work.

In turn, the part of you that exists outside the office helps bolster you and offers the strength needed to survive at work. In your home life, you have a much higher degree of autonomy than you do professionally. You can come closer to being the person you want to be, and you have got power over most of the decisions that affect you. There is a reciprocity in that environment that is absent on the job: No matter how much you love your work, it cannot love you—but the people at home *can*. Your personal life can therefore serve as a satisfying refuge from work, offering a sense of control and reward. It can balance the ups and downs of life in the professional world—but only if it stays protected and immune.

Distinguishing between who you are at home and who you are at work also helps you approach each place more effectively. You can develop skills vital to your professional life that are irrelevant in your personal one, and vice versa. Several years ago, I launched a major study of entrepreneurs across the last century, men such as Henry Ford, Andrew Carnegie, and Sam Walton. As I examined their careers, several common traits emerged, important characteristics that helped these men attain their phenomenal successes. For example, each was able to boil down the value of his product to a catchy, clear slogan. Ford said of his Model T: "It takes you there and it brings you back." George Eastman, founder of Eastman Kodak, said of his company's cameras: "You push the button and we do the rest." Complete simplification and clarity are invaluable to the entrepreneur.

Such a trait, however, would be worthless in your personal life, which is lived in a different sphere than business. A slogan that lets you connect powerfully to potential customers will never help you achieve communion with another human being. Intimate relationships with your family and friends are full of subtlety, feeling, and sensitivity. The depth of communication needed in those relationships is in a separate category entirely from the way you communicate at work. And that is merely one of a million instances in which the skills and outlook you need in one area simply do not translate to the other. So there is a benefit to thinking of the two arenas as separate and developing tailored approaches to each.

DO NOT GET ME WRONG. I'm not suggesting you completely polarize your identity, or advocating that you live your life in a way that is artificial. Neither do I believe you should check your personality at the office door. Having that degree of separation is something I do *not* admire, I do not think works, and in fact can be quite dangerous. For by taking the distinction to the extreme—by putting up a brick wall between the two spheres of your life rather than a screen—you run the risk of becoming two completely different people.

To illustrate both the possibilities and the pitfalls of the distinction I am suggesting you make, let me take two examples—and not from the classroom or theoretical workplace, but from the very pinnacle of the business profession. In my study of entrepreneurs, I examined not only the careers but also the personal lives of my subjects, giving careful consideration to whether and how each drew the kind of distinction I have described. Two, Eastman and Carnegie, drew definite boundaries between their work and personal identities. But while Eastman developed a work persona *like* who he was, Carnegie did not: His two selves became utterly divided, as if he were two different men.

Eastman, whose introduction of the one-dollar Kodak Brownie camera in 1900 transformed photography from an arcane science to a popular pastime, evidently gave the identity question some thought, as he came to his own firm conclusion. "What we do during our working hours determines what we *have*," he said, and "what we do in our leisure hours determines what we *are*." In the business arena, Eastman was intensely competitive and demanding, cutting off other firms from suppliers and sometimes working employees until they dropped. In his personal life, he was a reticent figure, devoted to his elderly mother. Yet while he approached his work and his play in completely different ways, those two selves were consistent—they were not at war with each other. His underlying values—such as his generosity—remained constant across both. When Eastman Kodak reached profitability, he distributed a large chunk of the earnings to his workers, unsolicited; in his private life (unlike many successful early-career entrepreneurs) he was an active and deep-pocketed supporter of many nonprofit institutions, including the University of Rochester, MIT, and the Eastman School of Music. Thus, even while keeping a hard distinction between his work and personal selves, Eastman maintained congruence and commerce between the two.

However, the man Carnegie was in his personal life and the man he was in his business life were not *like* each other at all. In fact, they bore little resemblance. In the private sphere, Carnegie vigorously espoused values that he utterly ignored professionally.

In his personal writings, Carnegie referred to the "debasing worship of money" and to the positive force of organized labor. But professionally, he authorized the use of any means—including violence—to bar unions from his own plants, keeping wages deliberately low and his own profits deliberately high. Personally Carnegie was humane and liberal, a connoisseur of literature and philosophy; in the business world, he was union-breaking and ruthless. Instead of putting up a permeable boundary between his personal and professional worlds, he had completely walled the two off, and the two had become incompatible. Stepping through the office door, Carnegie did not adopt a different *persona*—he became a different *person*.

OF COURSE, neither man's story is entirely cut and dried. Eastman's cannot be used as a purely admirable example, nor Carnegie's as a purely cautionary one. Both men defy categorization: Carnegie may have been a ruthless businessman, but ultimately became the century's greatest and most generous philanthropist; Eastman may have determined who he was by his leisure hours, but he had difficulty enjoying them ("I didn't smile," he noted, "until I was forty"). But what these stories do offer is contrast: one work/self distinction created well, and one created poorly.

Equally important, these stories demonstrate that the struggle to draw a distinction between your work self and real self is not unique to the early part of your career, but continues your entire professional life, regardless of how much money, success, or power you enjoy. Whether you are in the first few years of working or nearing retirement, separating who you are from what you do is an extremely difficult balancing act to perform—but ultimately, it is one that is *worthwhile*. George Eastman put it perfectly when a woman told him that she admired his ability to be hard in his business dealings. "One has to be hard in this world," he replied, "but one must keep one part of one's heart a little soft."

A Matter of
Black and White

Thomas K. McCraw

THOMAS MCCRAW is the Isidor Straus Professor of
business history at Harvard Business School. Prior to
joining the Harvard faculty, he earned a doctorate from
the University of Wisconsin and taught at the University
of Texas.

A prolific scholar, he is the author of *American Business, 1920–2000: How It Worked*, editor of *America Ver-
sus Japan*, and co-author of *Management Past and Pre-
sent*, among numerous other works. In addition to his
own research and teaching, he also serves as editor of the
Business History Review and lectures widely in the U.S.
and abroad.

In 1985, his book *Prophets of Regulation* won a
Pulitzer Prize.

✑ ✑ ✑

"Look at that goddamned Ike! Look at those fat-cat Republican bastards!" my father muttered, half to himself and half to his friends as they sat clustered around the television set in our small living room, watching Walter Cronkite announce the election returns.

My father and his colleagues had valid reason to be upset. Dwight Eisenhower was about to become the first Republican president in twenty years, and the Tennessee Valley Authority—the organization my father had worked for during his entire career, and which was a pure product of the Great Depression and of Roosevelt's New Deal—had yet to cope with a Republican White House. Nobody within the TVA had any idea what Ike might decide to do: Dismantle the entire organization? Put it under private-sector control? Find another way to throw a wrench into what had been its highly effective program of electrifying and providing flood control to the rural South? Whatever happened, they knew it wouldn't be good.

As it turned out, they were wrong. There was no catastrophe. Eisenhower appointed a man named Herbert Vogel, a capable general from the Army Corps of Engineers, as chairman. Vogel quickly saw what a remarkable organization the TVA was, went native — and everybody stopped worrying. In fact, under Vogel's management, the TVA had remarkable success, the capacity of its already-vast electrical power system more than doubling during his nine-year tenure.

But over the course of that November evening, while the certainty of a Republican victory rose, so did the palpable sense of panic in our household. As my parents and the other adults sat in the glow of our black-and-white TV, these changes were, literally, a matter of black and white.

AS A BUSINESS HISTORIAN, I study the ideas at the root of decision making for companies and government; I examine how those ideas drive strategy and action, and the results those actions bring. I look at how powerful, deeply held beliefs about how the world works — like my father's ideas about Eisenhower — shape business on both a large and small scale. For example, I've examined how ideas about competition have driven American regulatory policy and law. Ideas lead to policy, and policy drives real-life outcomes —

yet, as my father and his friends found out quite happily, even seemingly well-founded ideas can prove completely misguided.

As a business leader, *your* ideas will drive policies, and those policies will drive outcomes. It is critical, therefore, to truly understand your own ideas: to grasp how and why you have come to reason as you do. You must examine where your ideas come from, how they affect your view on the world, and where you may take a wrong turn by following them. To do so, you must examine your own past, and examine how those black-and-white beliefs and ideas were built.

To illustrate exactly what I mean, let me become a bit autobiographical myself. Let me tell you more about my own personal history, the foundation of my ideas, and my own process of reexamination.

I WAS BORN in the 1940s, but was really a child of the 1930s because of the powerful effect that the Great Depression had on my parents. Like most people who came of age during that era, they learned to scrimp and save on every conceivable thing, and for the rest of his life my father was reluctant to buy anything on credit.

In 1933, my father left his home in Florida for Norris, Tennessee, for the chance to work as an engineer on a dam and planned community being built there by the TVA, and for a salary of $75 a month. After working on Norris Dam for a couple of years, he moved on to a new town and a new project, a pattern that was to continue throughout his forty-year career. Throughout my childhood, my family lived a seminomadic existence. My brother and I attended many different schools, all of them in small towns that dotted Tennessee, Kentucky, and Alabama. Most of them were pretty awful.

During one four-year period I attended a tiny Catholic school in the remote mountains of East Tennessee, run by three nuns: Sisters Bernadelle, Grace, and Cecilia. It was something like a mission school in a developing country. Across eight grades were scattered approximately sixty students, in three rooms: what would today be referred to as "open classrooms." Instead of graduating from one class to the next, we usually just moved sideways to another row of seats, and after two or three years to another room. A few of the students, like me, came from middle-class homes and college-educated parents; some were Catholic, others Protestant; some were the sons and daughters of manual laborers within the TVA, and the rest were from poor local families. The nuns kept order by a fair amount of knuckle-rapping with yardsticks, and all of us who were Catholic were required to go to Confession every Friday, whether we needed to or not.

At the same time, I was also getting another kind of powerful schooling: that of the TVA itself, then a vibrant organization teeming with ambition and a seemingly bottomless pool of engineering talent from all over the world, capable of doing a construction project better than Brown and Root, Morrison Knudsen, Bechtel, or any other giant of the private sector. The TVA often rotated its crews as units, so that as my parents moved, so did my father's colleagues: building now a dam, then an electric power plant, then a new lock for an existing dam. Because each project was so enormous, demanded so much manpower, and was located out in the middle of nowhere, a sort of company town would spring up around each one. There would be rows of streets with perhaps twenty houses each: a substantial community, and one in which the standard de facto zoning by profession and by income did not occur. As a result, most of my friends were the sons and daughters of ironworkers, boilermakers, carpenters, millwrights, steamfitters, pipefitters, and brickmasons. It was not a genteel group: these were kids who ended up quitting school, joining the Marines or paratroopers, and coming back after two years with "Semper Fi", "Born to Raise Hell", or "Death Before Dishonor" tattooed on their arms.

Since the TVA was a large organization, with about forty thousand workers, my father moved up slowly through the ranks. Still, by his mid-forties, he was the construction superintendent in charge of building what was then the largest coal-fired power plant in the world. After that job was finished he was put in charge of building the highest single-lift lock in the world. This was over Wilson Dam in Alabama at Muscle Shoals, a lock six hundred feet long and over one hundred feet high. I remember, quite vividly, going down into the huge hole that was dug for the lock, looking up at the sides as the concrete was being poured, and simply being overwhelmed with the scale of it all: it was like seeing the Grand Canyon. To me, it seemed that the TVA was capable of creating an eighth wonder of the world.

THIS ENVIRONMENT was bound to leave deep impressions on a child, and it certainly gave me some other strong ideas. One, for example, was that labor unions were a good thing. All of TVA's craftsmen were organized into unions, all were well paid, and most of them were very committed to the job. The second was that the federal government, through this public corporation, could do things very well, in fact better, than the private sector. My father and his teams often brought in their big projects under budget, and they cut no corners. The New Deal, I believed also, was good; big organizations were good; big projects were good. On the other hand, the privately owned electric power industry was bad because it was so money-grubbing. Also, the Republican Party was bad, because it wanted to get rid of the TVA. All of those powerful prejudices were set by the time I was twelve and remained exactly as I have described them past my leaving home for college and indeed up through my twenties. So how did I—educated mostly in mediocre backwoods schools, and hardly a Socialist, but certainly a dyed-in-the-wool New Deal Democrat—end up spending the bulk of my career at Harvard Business School?

The study of history led me here—and it also led me to reexamine my own history, and the ideas and prejudices this history had produced. When I got to the University of Wisconsin for graduate school after four years as a naval officer, I was plunged into what I knew to be a truly topflight educational environment. Oddly, I soon realized that the best preparation I had had for graduate studies came from that tiny school in Tennessee. Sisters Bernadelle, Grace, and Cecilia were very smart and dedicated teachers, but I had never before thought of their little operation as first-rate. Yet from the vantage point of a graduate student, I realized that some of that Tennessee school's most striking characteristics, like its small size, were extremely advantageous. Every student was allowed to work at the level that his or her abilities permitted, and any intelligent and motivated kid could move forward much more quickly than in a standard academic setting. At the same time, the school had offered lessons in diversity: at an early age, I had to learn how to adapt myself to people of very different backgrounds, in an environment where almost no one was like me. Walking to school in the morning, through very poor neighborhoods, past evangelical churches and through an old-fashioned covered bridge had influenced how I saw myself and others and prevented me from growing up in a co-coon of familiarity. Later on, those kids in high school with the tattoos had merely furthered a valuable education, even if I hadn't realized it at the time.

While at Wisconsin, I became fascinated with the subject of business-government relations. Drawing on my own personal experience and first-hand knowledge, I wrote two books on the TVA. While I was doing the research, I found plenty of material for my work on the government side, but scant information from the private sector. As a historian, I was frustrated by that asymmetry and decided to accept a fellowship at Harvard Business School that would let me get access to better material from the private side. As I continued my work and research, it became increasingly apparent that the TVA had lost its edge during the 1970s after its glory years of the 1940s, '50s, and '60s. It no longer had access to the wonderful talent I remembered because there was now far more competition from the private sector and there wasn't the same sense of public service: people with top skills went to work for private enterprises at higher salaries and didn't feel called to work for the government. Private companies could now do the same jobs that the TVA used to, but often better.

Gradually the study of history—the field itself, as well as my own intersection with it—triggered my own self-examination, and that self-examination affected my study of the field, leading me to reconsider not just my past but also my focus in academia. I went from studying one organization—the TVA—to studying organizations more generally.

MY JOB AS A HISTORIAN is to better understand the past, to reevaluate it, and place it into a broader framework. In your professional life, you may not have the luxury of engaging in intense retrospection and historical analysis as often as I do. Yet it is imperative for you as a leader to understand where you—and by extension, your ideas—come from. You are a product of your time, your background, your parents, and your prejudices, and you must understand how each element from your past shaped your thinking in order to make the best decisions in the future. In other words, as you continue with your career, you must make strive to understand how you have come to reason as you do.

As the philosopher Kierkegaard said, we understand our lives only in retrospect—but must live them going forward. Without understanding your past, you cannot be effective in the future. If I still ran on my same old assumptions about the TVA, still saw it in black and white, I wouldn't be correct, and certainly wouldn't be a good historian. The TVA has changed, the world has changed, and so my own reasoning must change, too.

Don't let yourself settle into one way of seeing the world—reject that black-and-white lens. Look at your past, get autobiographical, understand why you think the way you do. Help yourself to make good decisions by seeing—and understanding—the color in between.

MANAGING
YOURSELF

A Bad Meal, and the Truth

Stephen P. Kaufman

STEPHEN KAUFMAN joined the school's faculty as a senior lecturer in business administration in January of 2001. He teaches the required first-year course in technology and operations management.

For fourteen years, he served as chief executive officer of Arrow Electronics, Inc., an NYSE-traded company. Prior to joining Arrow as a business unit head in 1982, he held executive positions at Midland-Ross Corporation and worked for global strategy-consulting firm McKinsey and Company, where he was elected partner in 1976.

A graduate of Harvard's M.B.A. program himself, he has returned to the school in part, he says, to "give back" by helping to train the next generation of leaders. It is a task he accomplishes not only in the formal classroom context, but also in office hours and casual conversations with his students, as he shares his own candid, commonsense observations on life in the business world.

G O LOOK in the mirror.

I mean that literally. Go stand in front of a mirror and look yourself straight in the eye. The man or woman you see staring back at you is the same one you're going to see one, ten, or even thirty years from now, when you're at the top of your organization.

Certainly, during that time you'll grow and develop in many ways: You'll have more experience and gray hair, for example, and your skills will get broader; your career interests may shift; and what seems most important today may not seem so tomorrow. But becoming a business unit head or CEO is no transforming thunderbolt. A lofty title in and of itself doesn't change you as a person.

What it *does* change, however, are your circumstances. The moment you become a senior manager, you'll be treated very differently than before. And one of the keys to being successful at the executive level is to be conscious of that treatment, and of how it affects you. You can't let it go to your head. You have to stay grounded and accessible.

I learned this lesson through an incident in my first really big management job as division president within a decentralized, diversified manufacturing company. For the first time in my life, I was the Boss. In my early days on the job, I hunkered down in my office to start familiarizing myself with how the unit operated: I looked at the P&L, the roster of key employees, and the performance targets for the year. In examining how the sales force was organized, something caught my attention: We had one office in St. Louis with five salespeople and another in Kansas City with three. Those cities are only a few hundred miles apart, and offhand I didn't see why we needed both. I assumed there was a good reason: Maybe there was a very high concentration of companies in that area that used our products, or maybe we had a big customer in Kansas City and needed a local link. Because the answer wasn't immediately apparent, I asked my VP of sales.

Two weeks later, I saw a memo from him posted on the bulletin board announcing that we had closed the Kansas City office, laid off two of the three salespeople, and transferred the third guy to St. Louis. I was stunned—I thought I had asked a *question*. Taking the memo off the board, I walked back to my office and my secretary's desk.

"Jan," I asked, mystified, "What happened? Why did we close the Kansas City branch?"

"Kurt said that you told him to close it," she said. "He assumed from your question that you wanted the office shut."

Now, Jan was a very smart and experienced professional secretary, and she had worked for each of the five division presidents over the past twenty-five years. As it gradually dawned on me where I had gone wrong, I knew she was probably one step ahead. "What would happen," I asked, "if on my way out of here today for a long lunch, I told you, 'I've been wondering how the office would look if the walls were painted green?'" She smiled. "When you came back two hours later," she answered, "you'd have green walls, and the painters would just be gathering up the drop cloths."

AT THAT POINT I realized that I was in an entirely new game, and it wasn't one for which I knew all the rules. My previous jobs and my business education had taught me most of the *skills* I needed to be division president: how to market a product, interpret the income statement, or solve a supply-chain problem. But nothing in my background had prepared me to take on the role itself. No one had explained to me that while I was still the same old Steve Kaufman as three weeks ago—same skills, same flaws, same sense of humor—the people I worked with were going to react to me entirely differently now because I was the Boss. No one had mentioned that my questions were going to be perceived as orders just because I had a fancy title and an office with a decent view.

Moving from employee to executive involves more than a change in status—it involves a major transition in how you're treated, in the fiber of your day-to-day life. As a regular rank-and-filer, you're used to working in a hierarchy, eating lousy airplane food, and constantly trying to please the guy up above. But when you become a senior manager—particularly a division or corporate president—something strange happens: The corporate world structures itself around *you*. You get great perks like an administrative staff, a company car, and first-class airline seats. You don't have to deal with unpleasant logistics, like trying to fix your own computer, because there are people around you striving to make sure your day-to-day life goes smoothly.

In addition to the material element is a human one: You get treated—and perceived—differently by those you work with. Employees interpret your questions as orders, almost always say "yes, that's a great idea" rather than pushing back or asking questions, fear your reactions and comments, and go to great lengths to shield you from bad news. A friend of mine summed up my later transition to CEO perfectly when he said, "Steve, there are two things you'll never get again—a bad meal, and the truth."

Of course, fine dining and good news are in and of themselves quite pleasant. Yet they have a negative effect on anyone in a senior management role. They cut you off from what's really going on inside the company, obscure the impact of your position, and diminish your effectiveness as a manager. When eating at five-star restaurants seems standard, it's easy to become self-important, to start imagining that life is really like this, or to think that your good treatment is due to who you are rather than to the job you happen to hold. When everyone around you bows and scrapes and tells you only what you want to hear, it's easy to become blind to the problems facing the corporation. You forget what it's like to be the junior guy, the low man on the totem pole, and you lose touch with people who run the business on the ground, facing those problems day to day. Wrapped up in your protective little CEO cocoon, you stop recognizing the impact of your position and title and start believing what you're told without applying critical judgment. And when all of that happens, your organization is going to have bigger problems than green walls.

In retrospect, I was lucky to go through the Kansas City incident when I did. Early in my career, before I began to take the perks for granted and become a victim of the white-glove treatment, I was forced to think, hard, about my new position. The experience demonstrated the new role's effect on me, on the people I was supposed to manage, and ultimately on the business itself. And I realized that if I didn't want to have any more unintended office closures—or worse—I needed to develop a plan to get beyond my office (in both the literal and figurative senses), stay grounded, and remain accessible to my employees. And I needed to do it fast.

On the personal side, I had to remember that while I now had the big-time job, I once was down at the bottom of the pyramid. I wasn't any different now than I had been then, and I'd better remember what I used to think about the pronouncements, memos, speeches, and videos I saw from the Big Boss. I shouldn't suddenly start believing my own BS, and needed to seem more human around people like Kurt—not to mention the guys out in Kansas City. And on the institutional side, I had to create a culture that encouraged open interchange across levels, in which people could ignore the chain of command, disagree, and bring company problems out into the open so they could get fixed. The workplace needed to function so that I and the people running things at the nuts-and-bolts level had free access to each other.

During my next few months at the company, I started developing a strategy to do just those things. Over time, as division head and later as CEO, I continued to hone my skills and tactics. And as *you* look ahead into your own career, I suggest you start honing them, too.

TO KEEP A SOLID GROUNDING and not get too swayed by the good treatment I got at work, I used one of the best resources available to me: I listened to my family. Now, your home life may not seem a natural environment in which to sharpen your business skills, but in this particular instance, it is. Nothing brings you down to earth as quickly and effectively as spending time with your spouse and kids. In that regard, I was fortunate: My wife was always willing to remind me that while I may have been lord and master of all I surveyed at the office, at home I was just the guy who took out the garbage on Tuesdays and picked up the dry cleaning on Saturdays. It's difficult to get too impressed with yourself when you're taking out trash or shoveling snow each weekend. Children, particularly teenagers, are also effective tools in this regard. Between the ages of twelve and twenty-five, your kids think that you're both dumb and embarrassing. Those years are likely to be ones in which you're hitting your full stride professionally. As you reach senior positions, it will be helpful to have an adolescent around to deflate your self-importance with a roll of the eyes, a prolonged sigh, or a caustic comment. Spending time with your family—and perhaps certain very close friends—is one of the most effective means of staying immune to "CEO disease."

Which, in turn, will form the basis for what's needed on the professional side: first, a few key colleagues willing to disagree with you. To be truly successful as a leader, you must have people around you who will challenge you, argue with you, and disagree with you. But it is incumbent upon you, the leader, to make this happen. You must bring people in who have the intellectual honesty and the emotional courage to do this, and then you must encourage them to do so. This means, for example, that when people push back at you or raise uncomfort-able issues, you need to thank them publicly for doing so and visibly give serious consideration to their concerns, rather than reacting with impatience or blowing them off with a frown, scowl, or sharp re-joinder. It's good if they can disagree without being disagreeable, but it is critical that they be willing to disagree.

Second, you need accessibility to the frontline troops. There's been much attention given to the idea of "management by walking around," to man-agers putting themselves on the same plane as their employees, but there's been relatively little advice on how to actually execute it. Meandering around the office and talking to people doesn't come natu-rally to everyone, and doing it the wrong way can backfire. One of our executives used to walk around the building with a frown of concentration on his face, head down, forgetting to greet people as he passed their desks. As a result, he got the reputation of being unapproachable, and he made middle managers skittish: Seeing a senior guy coming down the hallway looking that unhappy, they assumed budget cuts and layoffs weren't far behind. I didn't want to have the same effect. I wanted people to talk to me, rather than being scared off by my title, so I developed certain habits of getting out of my office, seeming more friendly, and spending time with employees in a more natural setting.

To make myself less intimidating, I took my jacket off and rolled up my sleeves when I left my office, and let myself look a little rumpled. And I went to where employees spent their time, rather than expecting them to come to me. I ate in the company cafeteria as often as possible, and *not* with other executives. I would find a table where I didn't know everyone and take my tray over. Since no one would get up if I was still eating—I remember people lingering over a slice of pie for forty minutes—I'd look for a table where people were just starting their meal.

Of course, as soon as I sat down everyone would tense up. So to break the ice I'd crack a joke at my own expense: *Did you see that memo? Geez, I wish I could write in English. My third-grade teacher would be embarrassed!* A little self-deprecating humor goes a long way. Then I'd try to ask about people's lives, their children, their passions outside work—and to be genuine, I had to be specific: *Is it your first child? Do you know yet if it's a boy or a girl? What are you hoping for?* The goal was to demystify me and get people to open up. After some small talk, I'd ask gentle but probing questions about their work. Had they even seen my memo? Were my messages reaching everyone? Were there ways to save money in their departments? I tried to find out if they were happy with and in the organization, and looked for insights that could be used to improve and strengthen it.

And I didn't limit my mingling to meals: I wanted to be accessible outside my office a short time in the middle of each day. So that I couldn't get too wrapped up in my own work and forget what I needed to do, I asked my assistant to remind me, nag me, and even schedule me to get out of the office, even if it was only to walk to the end of the building and back. And I put a yellow Post-it note on the inside of my doorjamb that said "Smile." As I walked around I'd stop, stick my head in people's cubicles, and say hello. When I saw a candy jar or donut box on a desk or table I'd stop, grab a piece, and talk for a few minutes. If there was a conference-room birthday party I'd stop in for cake and some casual conversation. Eventually, I didn't have to be reminded to walk around; it became folklore that I liked chocolate snacks, and I was invited to stop by when a department was having any kind of celebration. My methods became habit, and self-reinforcing.

IF YOU CAN MASTER these techniques and use them consistently, they will have a powerful effect on your business in a bottom-line way. Problems will filter up through the organization, and if you yourself have made poor choices as a manager, you'll hear about that, too. A case in point: As CEO I determined that the various operating units and staff departments of the company should be charged for use of the marketing communications department's services. I didn't want our managers constantly asking the advertising group to "pretty up" simple presentations or organize small meetings just because it looked like a free service. Great idea—in principle. Some time later, I was at lunch in the cafeteria with several middle managers, one of whom told me that the advertising department, which owned all the audiovisual equipment, was actually charging other groups $300 a day for use of their slide projectors for internal meetings. As a result, managers were going out and renting projectors from Kinko's, because it was cheaper than using the ones the company already owned. Each individual department kept their expenses down, but the company's were going up— needlessly. When I heard that, my blood pressure shot up about a thousand points. My own brilliant idea had led to an idiotic consequence. But because I had cultivated a relationship with someone lower down in the organization, she could bring it up to me, challenge me on the policy, and say, *Steve, is this* really *what you meant?*

SOME OF THESE METHODS I'm suggesting may feel self-conscious or even manipulative at first: walking around, making friendly chitchat, eating birthday cake—all with the calculated agenda of managing better. But that's how we all *learn*, through mindfulness and practice. It's like golf: When you first learn how to swing a club, you're thinking about every move, keeping your elbow straight, arms back, head down, twisting your body, rotating your hips. Or tennis: You're remembering to take a step, keep your eye on the ball, get low, follow through. In business, you're memorizing the techniques of connecting with people, staying grounded, being down to earth and approachable. At first you go through it mechanically—but then it becomes natural and, as with sports, you forget about the individual steps and just let it flow. And that same process of self-education should occur all the way through your career.

Wherever you are in your life right now—whether you're just out of college, a middle manager, or a CEO already—you can practice, train, and *learn* how to be a better leader.

Reunion

David E. Bell

DAVID BELL serves as chair for Harvard Business School's marketing department and for two of its executive education programs. An expert in retailing, he teaches a second-year elective course in the subject, and his scholarly work in the area has included an investigation into the interplay of pricing, inventory, and location strategies for multisite merchants.

In addition to his work in retail and marketing, he has done extensive research on risk assessment and analysis, examining—among other issues—how the psychological underpinnings of risk taking shape business choices. He has coproduced a series of books on the subject, including *Decision Making Under Certainty*, *Decision Making Under Uncertainty*, and *Risk Management*.

He earned his Ph.D. from the Massachusetts Institute of Technology and his undergraduate degree from Merton College, Oxford.

In the classroom he holds forth with his signature sarcastic wit.

A FEW YEARS from now, you'll receive a mailing from the School: a cheery letter asking you back for your fifth reunion. It will describe the dinners and parties planned for that weekend, and it will be filled with glossy color photos of alumni at reunions past, wearing clothes with the school logo on them, smiling enthusiastically.

Don't go.

If I have only one piece of advice to give you, it's that. Plan *ahead* on staying home.

A fifth reunion is a dangerous event. It forces you to take stock of what you've accomplished in the short period since graduation, and to evaluate it on relative, rather than absolute, terms—to grade your achievements and earnings against those of your peers, instead of against your own career goals or standards of success. Pulling into the campus parking lot before that "welcome back" dinner, you'll find yourself squinting around anxiously at the makes and models of the other cars, trying to figure out how well your classmates have done since graduation day, and how well you've done in comparison. At the "get reacquainted" cocktail party, you'll stand there awkwardly with your gin and tonic silently calculating how you measure up, as you hear which members of your class have become senior vice presidents, or millionaires. The whole event will provoke an enormous amount of anxiety, unproductive worry about your professional success and net worth.

But what's worse, the mere prospect of a reunion five years off can affect the decisions you make *today*. Even while still in school, you anticipate the envy you'll feel when parking your battered old Ford between two gleaming BMWs, or your own regret and disappointment when admitting to former classmates now in high-powered jobs that the company you founded failed. As a result, you'll begin, consciously or not, managing your life *toward* the reunion—gearing your career to what's most likely to yield a notable résumé entry in the short term, or to make heaps of money quickly. You'll shelve whatever aspirations you have that aren't certain to pan out fast and take work that can pay for a fancy car but that you don't actually *want* to do. You'll lose sight of your professional goals, of what's really important to you. You'll become overly wary of making risky decisions about your career — or of making any important decisions about it at all.

As a professor, I've seen this happen with my students over and over again. Afraid they'll be struggling along, poor and unaccomplished, when their friends from school have made it big, new graduates take the securest-seeming possible routes, the jobs with the highest starting salaries, so that — metaphorically at least — they can come back to reunion in style. Students who yearn for the creativity of media careers go into investment banking; others who long for the autonomy and adrenaline of start-up life join staid corporations. Imagining what their classmates will have been able to achieve in five years — the corner offices, enormous bonuses, and lofty titles — they've become excessively averse to risk, afraid to follow their own interests for fear of coming up empty-handed. And the result? Lots of intelligent, talented people spending time in impressive-sounding, lucrative careers that suit them poorly and do nothing to help get them toward where they really want to go.

Of course, it's not only M.B.A. students or those of us with a fifth reunion looming who are risk-averse. Everyone is to some degree. We all hesitate before making a significant career change (or for that matter when staring down the barrel of any other major life decision, such as getting married or choosing where to live). And we do so for largely predictable reasons. Many of us feel we haven't got the right expertise to apply in a new line of work; we haven't got the self-confidence to try it out; we haven't got enough money in the bank to fall back on if we fail. Some of us have a history of bad luck and always see our chances for success as slim. Others of us have a deep fear of the unknown, or have never developed a taste for the enormous upside— the money, job satisfaction, or other payoff—that taking the right risk brings. Alone, any one of those factors can create a serious case of risk-aversion— and unfortunately, it's one that the thought of attending a reunion makes all the more acute.

Luckily, however, this affliction is treatable. By learning to reframe the way you think about risk, you can recalibrate your tolerance for taking it. And the very first step toward doing so is to make a firm resolution to chuck that invite letter—no matter how cheery—straight into the bin, and to forgo your fifth reunion. For that matter, skip the tenth, too.

The fifteenth?

Bag it.

KNOWING HOW to take professional chances, and take them without undue worry, is something I've learned by reflecting on my own experiences, and on one decision in particular. For while today I might preach at you about risk taking from inside a cozy little office, I didn't get here without taking a few gambles myself.

Twenty-five years ago in England, when I was just out of Oxford, I decided to go to graduate school abroad. Plucking out a map of North America, I scanned for cities I had heard of—Boston, New York, Toronto, Philadelphia—and sent away for information on universities there. Because I had absolutely no money at the time, I applied to, and ended up attending, the only school that offered foreign students a waiver of the application fee.

At the time, that move should have seemed a highly risky one. There I was, heading to a new country, penniless, to an institution I had selected for the sole purpose of saving twenty-five dollars. Yet looking back, my venture paid off: I wouldn't now be in Boston, or a professor at Harvard, if I hadn't taken that route. And because I employed, however unwittingly at the time, three essential strategies—

constructive though unorthodox ways of thinking about risk—I was able to go forward.

First, I was honest about the specific types of rewards I sought from my work, on what I wanted in exchange for doing my job, a certain kind of prestige and flexibility, and I focused on the career path most likely to offer me both. As an academic I knew I would never become fabulously wealthy (and indeed, would make much more money in any number of other professions), but that I would be compensated in the ways that were important to me. At dinner parties when I told people I was a university professor, they would *ooh* and *aah* and act impressed; day to day, besides the hours spent in the classroom, I would have near-total discretion in how I spent my time. Aware that I'd have to get a Ph.D. in order to become a professor, going off to graduate school didn't seem a risky move in the least, but the surest, safest, and perhaps *only* way to get me toward my goals and a career in which I'd be satisfied.

Second, I was willing to accept a wide range of outcomes to my choices. Applying to graduate school in America, I was ready to live in many different cities, not setting my heart on any one particular school, and ready to accept a variety of professional results. My criteria for success were broad: to do research in the subjects that interested me, and in a relatively comfortable environment. Because I wasn't fussy about details, the move itself didn't seem as fraught with risk.

As a rule the more *specific* you are in any of your given ambitions, the more risky the idea of pursuing them becomes; as your objectives narrow, the number of potential pitfalls in pursuing them rises. If my sole aim in coming to the United States had been to gain the presidency at Harvard, the whole endeavor would have appeared very chancy indeed. I would have been put off at the start by my high probability of later failure, and the high likelihood of my disappointment in the end. Ninety-nine percent of the time, when people see a career path as too risky, it's because they're being insufficiently flexible in their goals. Many of my students hesitate to become entrepreneurs, for instance, for fear they won't become Bill Gates. By defining success only as dominating an industry and making billions, they've made the whole venture seem too improbable, and therefore hazardous, to ever begin.

Third, as I readied to sail off to parts unknown, I took a long-term view. I had decades to accomplish what I wanted, and in the context of whole *decades*, my choice of where to go to graduate school looked much smaller and less significant. Creating a career as an academic — much less a well-respected or well-known one — is no overnight proposition; it takes fifteen years at least merely to get a Ph.D. and come up for tenure. And that far-off time horizon for success appears in most managerial careers as well. Becoming CEO of any company doesn't happen right away; starting one yourself can involve years of frustration before you gain any traction, not to mention success. Risk-averse people (and reunion-goers) worry about the short term, about what will yield results in a flash. But looking at the whole scope of your career at once, and realizing that even the most chancy decision will seem small in the whole sweep of it, enables you to take far more risk.

Of course, these strategies aren't the *only* helpful ways of becoming more at ease with risk taking—there are other effective methods, too. You can associate with risk takers, for example, and hope the attitude is catching; you can practice taking many small risks at a time by playing Lotto (a method which may also provide a comfortable nest egg in case larger gambles don't pay off). But in my opinion and my experience, these three methods are the most direct and the most reliable.

EVEN AS YOU do what I'm suggesting—think of your job in terms of rewards, keep your definition of success broad, and take a long-term view—above all else, maintain a sense of *perspective* about your career. Don't take chances and then work so doggedly and endlessly toward having them work out that you make yourself miserable. Set a time limit on yourself. Become an inventor, an entrepreneur, or a circus performer, whatever you want to do—but don't spend years peddling a product that won't sell, working at a company that fails to flourish, or performing an act that no one watches. Think of those presidential candidates who pop up every election, seemingly oblivious to the fact they haven't a chance of winning, admirably striving for a risky goal, but throwing away years of their lives in the process.

My suggestion? Determine to take chances throughout your career, pick a number of years you're willing to wait for those chances to pay off, and after that time is up, throw in the towel. If you've arrived at a certain age, have taken multiple risks to get yourself into the plum position you want, but haven't been able to get there, retire. Forget about where you were trying to go, hit the golf course, and never look back.

Soon afterward, you'll get a cheery notice in the mail, inviting you back to your twenty-fifth reunion.

And *that* one, I think, you should attend.

On the Fallacy
of Perfection

Nancy F. Koehn

A graduate of Stanford University, NANCY KOEHN holds a master's degree in public policy and a doctorate in European history from Harvard. An expert in the areas of branding, business strategy, and customer relationships, she is the author of *Brand New: How Entrepreneurs Earned Consumers' Trust from Wedgwood to Dell*, a book that profiles six groundbreaking businesspeople who founded successful, enduring companies at moments of societal and economic upheaval. At HBS since 1991, she teaches courses in both entrepreneurship and business history.

Koehn appears frequently as a commentator on a range of television programs, from *Good Morning America* to *Biography*. With her cropped red hair and quick-fire speech, her enthusiasm about the subjects that intrigue her is contagious, whether she is in front of students, in her office, or on camera.

My FATHER was an academic, like me. A philosophy professor, he was a brilliant, demanding teacher who urged his students to think "carefully, deeply, and systematically" and to ask hard questions of themselves and of their world. He was incredibly energetic both inside and outside the classroom. Growing up, and indeed, well into adulthood, I saw him as someone uniquely capable of getting things *done* in the world. Even after he retired from teaching in the early 1990s, he continued to work with organizations ranging from the American Philosophical Association to the Sierra Club to the Society for Business Ethics. In these pursuits, as in his teaching, he was a highly principled person. Much of his philosophical research had centered on ethics, specifically business ethics, and he applied what he taught and wrote about—honesty, fairness, respect for others—to his academic, political, and charitable responsibilities.

My father died unexpectedly last summer. He was sitting at the kitchen table reading the *New York Times* one evening, and his heart failed. He slipped into a coma, and three days later he stopped breathing.

I loved my dad very much. In many respects—his values, his practical skills, his work, even his athletic ability—he had been a strong role model for me, and losing him has been a profoundly painful experience. It has also been a reckoning: with my father and his life, with death, and with myself. And in this reckoning, this engagement with issues and questions I had not before encountered, I have come to know great sadness, sadness that has brought me to my knees.

At the same time, my father's death also left me with several gifts, among them a newfound appreciation for what we, the living, really have. Like many Type A personalities, I have spent much of my time focused on what I lack, have not done, or need to do to try to bring about a certain kind of tomorrow. My father's passing has helped me to take stock now of what is, to realize that whatever is to come, I have today.

But his death gave me something else, too: the ability to see him in a much more *complete* way than I had been able to when he was alive. During my dad's lifetime, I could only view a few individual snapshots of him at a time: in one frame, the driven Phi Beta Kappa scholar; in another, the enthusiastic professor gesticulating at the blackboard and asking rapid-fire questions of his students; in another, him sitting in his favorite chair laughing loud and long over a political joke; in yet another, grumbling at the dinner table about a possible family outing.

But in the aftermath of his death, I wanted, I *needed*, to take all of my disparate experiences— conversations, correspondence, moments I spent with him, favorable and unfavorable impressions alike—and spread them out in my mind, lay all the photographs, so to speak, on the table. With all of the pictures of him before me, a truer image of my father emerges, one that is more real and thus more sustaining. I can see his strengths and achieve-ments—but I can also take in his weaknesses and his failures. His exuberance and professional dedication coexist with self-doubt and harshness. His energy in-termingles with occasional resentment. I can see the father I loved and continue to love: a man who was complicated, intelligent, and flawed.

This experience has been extremely powerful, allowing me to transcend the difficulties I had with him. But it has also had another effect. It has moti-vated me to try to look at other people, and at myself, in the same way I have been able to see my father: *from as many angles as possible simultaneously*, considering not only the positive qualities, the accomplishments and successes, but also what I call the "flabby" part of life, the imperfections and vulnerabilities, and everything in between.

In the process, I've realized that we live in a moment in which success is defined along one dimension: in terms of specific achievement, be it financial reward, power, fame, beauty, or a combination of these. We are rarely privy to the "flabby" parts of any successful person's life or to all the shades of gray between one's achievements and one's failings. After all, one can never be too rich or too thin, right? Or so the mantra goes. Isn't this how our moment spells success?

In the year since my father died, I have tried to understand why that is so: Why the ability to see anyone, particularly ourselves, as I can now see my dad—in a broader, more integrated and honest way—remains elusive. The difficulty, I think, stems from a deep discomfort with imperfection in a culture that encourages us to try to be perfect. We believe that we can be perfect and should be, that we must never stop striving to be perfect, and so we are embarrassed, disappointed—and exhausted—when, inevitably, we aren't.

In our society generally, and especially in the segment of it populated by high achievers, flaws are frowned upon, vulnerabilities forbidden. Consequently, these attributes are usually hidden. In some contexts, merely *acknowledging* a personal weakness or a business mistake—be it my father's diffidence or a senior executive's strategic misstep—is rare. And success, as it is so often defined, gets an extra coating of gloss: In both newspaper articles and cocktail party conversations, a person's accomplishments are often piled upon one another in descriptions ("She's not only a senior vice president, but an honors graduate of Stanford") as if each achievement alone painted an insufficiently perfect portrait of the achiever. Influenced by the media and its sound bite–quick judgments, we tend to view success as binary: either you have it, or you do not. We're used to seeing illustrious people, particularly those in business, depicted as consistently, unflaggingly successful. And this perspective has important consequences.

TO TAKE A SPECIFIC EXAMPLE: During the stock market run-up of the late 1990s the senior leaders of many dynamic, high-performing companies such as WorldCom were portrayed in the business press as iconic figures. Their firms grew rapidly as earnings rocketed up each quarter, and stock prices soared. Many wanted to imitate these executives, understand their wisdom, use their business models, and apply the magical recipe they seemed to have conjured up for success. Then, beginning in late 2000, this logic no longer seemed so valid. What had prevailed in the public mind as a virtuous cycle of organizational—and in some sense, cultural—success was revealed to be something far different. Many of those same managers were playing fast and loose with their companies' accounting practices, rewarding themselves handsomely at the expense of other stakeholders, running their businesses badly, and in some cases, breaking the law. In the end, they were not authentic leaders. Many were greedy, some exercised very poor judgment, and a few damaged their organizations beyond repair.

Part of our reaction to such revelations was a justifiable sense of betrayal at the dishonesty on display, not to mention at the losses employees and shareholders suffered from these executives' decisions. But another part of our reaction was shock that certain individuals who had been so recently lauded could have fallen so far, so fast. The peaks of perfection in our society are high, and the troughs of infamy are deep. In the last five years, we have ridden a roller coaster from irrational exuberance to irrational pessimism seemingly without any stops in between. Perhaps some of the disillusionment we are still experiencing about the last five years of business in this country is tied up with the roller coaster of success as it is currently defined. An individual, a company, an economy, it appears, can only be at the top of the hill or at the bottom of the valley. We embrace the view from the top. But we are not sure how to come to terms with the valleys (or with anything located below the summit of perfection).

Of course, the abdication of responsibility that characterized some business leaders' conduct during the recent past does not lurk beneath every achievement. Nonetheless, the example demonstrates how stubbornly we set our sights on perfection—on an all-encompassing, no-holds-barred embrace of specific people, organizations, ways of being.

AN EVEN BIGGER PROBLEM, however, is that we apply that same expectation to ourselves. Unrelenting success—being up at the top of that hill, all the time—becomes our barometer, the impossible but seductive standard against which we have to measure up. When we fall short—and invariably, we all do—and make mistakes or encounter failure, the result is a deep sense of shame, which can lead to a sense of overwhelming inadequacy. Like the collective perspective on a "fallen angel" company, we often swing from one extreme to another in our opinion of ourselves. Those feelings, produced by the inability to live up to our own mythologized view of success, can be corrosive. They are frequently draining and all-consuming, and they can prevent us from learning from our mistakes, seeing others and ourselves more realistically, and productively moving forward in our lives and in our careers.

Flawlessness, like worthlessness, in *any* human being is an illusion. The more we uncover about any particular person's life, no matter how perfect it seems at first glance, the more complicated we see that it really is. Alongside each positive personal trait, such as my father's intelligence, live vulnerabilities, like his diffidence. In a similar vein, an individual's weaknesses coexist with—are close neighbors of—his or her strengths. If we had the luxury of reading an unflinchingly honest biography of *any* very successful person—a politician, a polar explorer, a CEO—there would be not only paragraphs but whole *chapters* on their frailties and failures: stories of the lost election, the broken marriage, or all the deals that fell apart.

My academic research has been a petri dish for studying both successes and failures of high-achieving people—and the emotional fallout they often experience in moving from chapter to chapter in their lives. One of the entrepreneurs I've studied in depth is Henry Heinz, who was born in 1844. His life offers an important illustration of the interplay of triumph and struggle and its broader consequences for leaders. In 1869, Heinz founded a food processing company in Pittsburgh at a time when very few Americans ate food that they did not grow themselves. Heinz went on to revolutionize consumers' eating habits, producing pickles, condiments, and baked beans. (In the process, as one of my M.B.A. students put it, Heinz became the "ketchup king.")

But such enduring success did not come in a smooth, uninterrupted fashion. It involved traumatic setbacks. In 1875, Heinz's company failed. A national depression coupled with a credit crunch left the firm without sufficient operating capital. Heinz borrowed money for as long as he could. Within a few months, however, he had exhausted available resources. Angry creditors charged Heinz with fraud and had him arrested. The local sheriff placed a levy on Heinz's personal goods, his business assets, and his father's property. All of these goods were sold at a public auction, which the entrepreneur could not bear to attend. The food company closed down, and a week before Christmas declared bankruptcy.

Heinz's diary records his emotional reaction to the crisis. Depression, shame, and self-doubt haunted him. "No Christmas gift to exchange," Heinz wrote, adding that his wife "Sallie seemed grieved, and cried, yet said it was not about our troubles; only she did not feel well. It is grief. I wish no one such trials. . . . I feel as though people were all pushing us down because we are bankrupt." By the end of the month, Heinz perceived himself to be the object of sudden, widespread disapproval. "A man is nowhere," he noted in his diary, "without money."

Yet despite this enormous blow, Heinz found his way back to the food business and to a stronger sense of himself. Within a year, he had started another company, using funds borrowed from relatives and knowledge he had gained from failure. He went on to create first-rate products, a powerful brand, and a world-class organization that employed thousands and made significant contributions to the Pittsburgh community.

How did Heinz recover from potentially crippling failure? By taking stock of who he was, what he wanted, whom he cared for, and why things had gone so bad so fast for him and his business. This reflection, including a willingness on Heinz's part to sit with his own shame, seems to have had a profound effect on the entrepreneur, clarifying his own faith in himself and helping him learn from past mistakes.

Of course, it's one thing to hear that *other* people managed to move past guilt, self-recrimination, and embarrassment to bounce back after their own failures, and it's another to do it yourself. Merely accepting your own mistakes and shortcomings is very difficult, and moving past a personal sense of shame about them in order to learn from them is even harder. But, as Heinz's experience illustrates, it is essential to leading and living well.

IN 1991, another Harvard Business School faculty member named Roland C. Christensen published a book about teaching by the case study method titled *Education for Judgment*. I mention it because I think there is a lot captured in those words. As an aspiring leader, you want to make a difference in an organization and perhaps in the larger world—to add your own patch to the quilt of human activity and to make that patch as colorful and enriching as possible.

But to do that does not mean merely learning how to sew with a given stitch and the perfect needle, or having a sparkling toolbox of business skills suitable for very occasion. It involves something more elusive, more slippery, and—I suspect—potentially more powerful. Becoming a leader means learning to use your intelligence, integrity, and experience *to make sound judgments.* How you use the authority you will have, what you make of it and of yourself in the process must be at the core of your leadership mission and method. And helping you acquire an education, a way of thinking about these questions, not just now, but going forward into the rest of your life, is my primary goal in telling you this story.

I want to help prepare you to make good choices, good judgments, and not just in the realm of business—about marketing strategy, workforce retention, or venture capital financing—*but in the whole crazy quilt of life.* And I believe that without being able to look at yourself and the people around you honestly, warts and all, the likelihood of making those sound decisions goes way, way down.

So what I'm suggesting you do is perform a kind of personal accounting. Learn to consider your imperfections along with your strengths. Recognize your mistakes *without* becoming incapacitated by shame. Forget the tanned, toned, strong, high-earning, high-achieving, unrelentingly perfect person you think you're supposed to be. Learn to think of yourself and the people around you as "perfect" in the true dictionary definition of the term: not as flawless or beyond reproach—but as total, as lacking in no essential detail, as *whole*. And there's one simple way to do that.

Take all of your own memories and experiences and lay them out in your mind together, as if you were laying photographs out on a table. Let a new image of yourself emerge—a fuller image, an honest image, one of you in your entirety. See yourself as I now see my father: as someone who, like him, like me, like *all* leaders, is complicated, intelligent, flawed—and complete.

Katharine Hepburn and Me

Rosabeth Moss Kanter

ROSABETH MOSS KANTER is the Ernest L. Arbuckle Professor of Business Administration at Harvard Business School. Throughout her career, she has been a leader in management education and thought. A senior adviser to major companies and governments worldwide, she has received nearly two dozen honorary doctorates and is to date the author of sixteen books. In 2001, she received the Academy of Management's career honor for scholarly achievement and influence on the field. On the HBS faculty since 1986, she has also served as editor of the *Harvard Business Review* and as a tenured professor at Yale.

Despite her impressive accomplishments and regular work with senators and CEOs, however, she remains disarmingly down-to-earth.

～の～の～の

I N FEBRUARY 1978, New England had its worst
blizzard in a hundred years. Almost three feet of
snow fell in a storm that has become local legend.
The entire Boston metropolitan area came to a stand-
still for the better part of a week—roads were impass-
able, the airport was closed, and the public was ordered to stay home. The governor threatened to arrest
anyone who tried to drive. I was early in my career
as a professor and business consultant with my first
best-selling book, and I was scheduled to speak at
an American Management Association meeting in
Chicago the day after the worst of the storm. Getting
to Chicago was out of the question. I called the Association and said, "I'm sorry, I can't make it to the meeting." The people organizing the conference said, "You
have to come." And I said, "But I can't—the governor's orders." They said, "Well, maybe if you tell the
governor it's the American *Management* Association, he'll let you come." (As though *management*

was somehow above the rules—an attitude that I wanted to change.)

They were determined that there wasn't going to be a hole in their program, so we finally agreed that I would give the speech by telephone; in the days before videoconferencing, this was the best that we could do. I thought, *this is very weird. Giving a speech to a small piece of black plastic is going to be pretty disconcerting.* So I invited a few friends over to my house in Cambridge to listen, give me feedback, and make the whole experience seem a little more natural.

When the time came for the speech, my friends arrived, some of them on cross-country skis. I dialed the number I had been given and waited to hear my introduction.

Silence.

No introduction, no operator, and since it was a one-way line, no sound from the audience. So I dove right in.

"Since none of you can see me," I started, "I will begin by describing myself. I look just the way most of you imagine someone in my position ought to look—tall, willowy, and like a younger Katharine Hepburn."

I couldn't hear any response from Chicago, but the people in my living room laughed, and I relaxed.

Their reaction gave me the confidence to sail through the forty-five minute talk. I had been told that some-one would get back on the line at the end and say thank you. Again: silence. I was left holding what felt like a dead telephone. (At that time, people in management often forgot their thank yous — another item on my change agenda.) When I hung up, satis-fied I had done a good job under the circumstances, my assembled friends applauded the speech and es-pecially the disarming opening comment.

NOW, I SHOULD tell you — my speech's opening, while humorous, was not entirely accurate: I'm not 5'9," I don't have perfectly sculpted cheekbones, and when I plop into an armchair I look comfortable but hardly insouciant. In fact, my picture was on the convention brochure, so many of the people in the Chicago crowd already knew what I looked like. But by defying my audience's expectations in that unique and humorous way, I accomplished some serious objectives. I swept awkwardness and distrac-tions off the table, got my audience to listen and to focus, and shone the spotlight directly on what really mattered — on the *substance* of what I had to say. And in doing so, I reinforced a theory I've developed about effective leadership.

While my Katharine Hepburn line may have sounded casual, it was not an ad-lib. I had given it careful consideration that snowy morning as I planned how to overcome the dual obstacles facing me. In those days, I was still starting out—a baby professor, a baby consultant—and there were virtually no other women in my field. On top of that, my audience was a thousand miles away, and I knew it contained people who were unhappy with me for not strapping on snowshoes and trekking out there. To get that tough group to perceive me as in charge and as worth listening to, I had to build a bridge that would span the gap in age, gender, and geography—and I had to do it quickly. And with my favorite movie star's help, I did.

Knowing that the image most people had of a successful woman was close to Katharine Hepburn—smart as a whip and beautiful to boot—I used that preconceived image to my advantage. I surprised my listeners, piqued their interest, and made them laugh (both at my joke and at themselves). I relaxed them, bonding them to me and to each other. I sent the message that what I looked like—or how I couldn't be seen—wasn't important, but that what I had to say *was*. By defining myself on my own terms and addressing uncomfortable issues directly, I took control of the situation and got my audience ready to concentrate on the content of my speech.

Does that sound like a lot for two sentences to accomplish? Perhaps, but I've seen CEOs, politicians, and leaders in every field do this over and over again: come into a situation and, with one or two well thought-out remarks, take charge. This ability is one of the hallmarks of leadership. Effective leaders go out ahead of other people to define a situation, transcending barriers and shifting attention away from distractions and differences. They communicate what they want to accomplish and why—all in a way that people can relate to, that motivates other people, and that makes it easy for others to listen and act. Leaders close the gaps that might separate them from their audiences, making sure that they build bridges and create receptivity for their ideas. And they do all this with the power of *voice*.

By "voice" I mean a person's ability to create a solid connection with people he or she may have just met and to communicate to a group that he or she has something worth hearing. The first challenge of leadership is commanding attention, and generally you have only a few brief minutes to get it. During the blizzard, the only tool I had to reach my audience was my *literal* voice, the one carried over the phone wire. Because I knew that the audience might find listening to a disembodied speaker bizarre, and perhaps a little off-putting, I had to maximize the power of my leadership voice: to focus on exactly what I said, how I said it, and what impact I could achieve.

I knew that my voice had been heard—in this case both literally and figuratively—when, in the months after my telephone address, after the snow had cleared and I was able to travel, people would come up to me at meetings with big smiles on their faces and say, "You look *just* like Katharine Hepburn!" And I would answer, "Chicago! You were there!" And since then, I have often used that same voice—and sent that same message—and not only in front of large groups, but also one-on-one. I remember being met at an airport, looked over, and told, "We expected a taller person." I answered, "Well, I think very tall thoughts, and I do my best work sitting down." The voice I used was funny, lighthearted, and nonaggressive. It brought us closer, but it also established my self-confidence and command of the situation. Leaders who are comfortable with themselves help others relax and listen. Leaders do not have to be loud to seem powerful; I've seen some very effective chief executives speak with a quiet, understated force. Yet despite differences in style, the goal is always the same: to clear away all the roadblocks standing between the group and the pressing issues at hand.

WHEN I TEACH young business students as well as seasoned executives, the advice I give is the same: Find a leadership voice that works for you, is true to who you are—and *use* it. Of course, that doesn't mean you should always be talking. Quite the contrary: One of the key tasks of leadership is to listen to others, and to listen well. But wherever you are in your career right now—whether you find yourself presenting reports you've written to vice presidents, walking into conference rooms full of managers for meetings, hitting the road to raise money for your venture or your cause, or striding up to a podium to deliver a keynote address— what you *do* say needs to get through, to have a real and special impact. Leadership demands that you set the agenda, define a direction, shape a vision, and rally people to work with you to change the world. But first, you must win them over.

When you enter any meeting or event, whether it is with ten people you know or ten thousand you don't, be aware that you have a very short time to create the appropriate impression and shape the situation. Other people have assumptions you need to dispel, and your goal is to establish yourself and the bonds between you and the other people quickly and clearly. For Chicago, the particular gulf I had to bridge was geographic, technological, and demographic. You may have to overcome different barriers—ones of culture, for example, or self-interest. You may find yourself working on a team in one of your organization's foreign offices, or sitting across the negotiation table from people whose goals differ vastly from your own. No matter what the situation, the burden is on you as a leader to establish common ground and develop a working rapport while presenting yourself as you want to be seen.

To do so effectively, tailor your strategy to the specific situation; sensitivity to your surroundings is crucial. Before you give a speech or a report or a proposal, for example, research the composition of the audience—who they are in terms of age, gender, experience; whether they are laypeople or professionals; if they have traveled very far to the conference; or if you are the last speaker before lunch. You have to know who your audience is and what they are there for, but also, less tangibly, you have to read the mood of a gathering—and if that mood is negative or awkward, you have to find a way to turn it around.

Yet as much as you want to win over your audience, never pander, condescend, or change yourself too much. Assume your audience is intelligent, sincere, and hungry for fresh ideas and insights. You want to bring them to you—on your terms, to hear your own distinctive voice. By all means borrow from those you admire, but never try to be someone you are not; have your voice be powerful, but always be your own. And know that if you can laugh at yourself, your power will not be diminished. It will grow.

Finally, remember the other lessons of that Chicago speech. Surround yourself with supporters who share a smile with you during tough challenges—people who will be there for you, even if they have to arrive on skis. Find the courage to speak though a storm rages around you, or when it seems like no one could possibly be listening. And be ready to invoke alter egos that fit whatever situation you must master, models you can draw on to get the audience on your side.

TWENTY-FIVE YEARS after orating into that silent phone line to Chicago, and too many speeches to count later, I'm a full professor with an endowed chair and research staff, the number of women in business has skyrocketed, and if we have heavy snow in Massachusetts, I can speak via videoconference to almost anywhere in the world. But I still use my voice in the same way, for the same purposes: to bridge gaps and create focus—to *lead*.

And for those of you who are wondering, I *still* look like a young Katharine Hepburn—or maybe these days, more like Jodie Foster.

LEADING
OTHERS

Sara's Story

H. Kent Bowen

KENT BOWEN joined the Harvard Business School faculty in 1992 as part of the technology and operations management unit. For more than twenty years he was a professor at the Massachusetts Institute of Technology, where he cofounded Leaders for Manufacturing, a collaborative education and research effort between the schools of engineering and management. He holds both a bachelor's degree and a doctorate in engineering, the former from the University of Utah and the latter from MIT.

He speaks in a deliberate manner, each unhurried phrase underscoring the careful thought behind it. Yet his quintessentially professorial demeanor and methodical intelligence is accompanied by an avuncular warmth. Students frequently seek him out for advice on academics, career, and life.

A S A GIFTED, ambitious, and hard-working person, you will ascend the ladder of success. Perhaps one day you will lead a division of the organization you work in—or the entire organization itself. Yet as you move up in the ranks and find yourself with greater power, you will also increasingly be confronted with tough decisions—ones that affect the lives and the livelihoods of other people. Maybe your company will have a reorganization, and you will need to lay people off.

Each person that you fire—the factory worker, engineer, janitor, or manager—may be invisible to you. She may work in an area of the company you seldom consider, and you may not even know her name. Life may have handed him different circumstances than it handed you, and perhaps he has made different choices than you would have made in his place.

Let me tell you about one of these people. Her name is Sara.

ALTHOUGH SHE DID not grow up in a rich or well-connected family, or with any of the other advantages which smooth the way toward success, Sara was intelligent, enterprising, and resourceful. What she accomplished early in life was due to her own talents and efforts.

Raised on her family's small Utah farm, throughout her childhood Sara would rise at dawn to put in a few hours helping with chores before she left for school. Born left-handed in an era when there was still a stigma attached to this trait, she applied her considerable determination to becoming ambidextrous and for the rest of her life was able to use her right and left hands with equal ease and proficiency. She loved school and became a particularly avid reader, devouring two to three books every week; by the time she was a teenager, she had read every book in the town's library. Even after skipping two grades of school, she managed to graduate as class valedictorian.

Sara's skills didn't end with farmwork and homework, however. She was also creative, teaching herself to crochet, knit, and sew. Sitting at her family's kitchen table with a large basketful of cloth scraps, she could quickly assemble intricate patchwork quilt patterns without benefit of any preexisting design, relying only on her own sense of color, space, and symmetry.

When she was fourteen Sara became a business-woman, taking over the management of a small herd of her father's cows. On top of her accelerated school schedule and daily farm duties, she assumed respon-sibility for the animals' health and welfare, budget-ing for their feed and milking them twice a day. She marketed the milk to and negotiated prices with local dairy processors and kept the books for the entire en-terprise, which, unsurprisingly, was profitable. But rather than keeping the money she earned for her-self, Sara helped pay tuition for three older brothers already in college.

Had her circumstances and her life choices been different, Sara's smarts and hard work could have led her to enormous professional success. She might have become a lawyer or doctor, a university profes-sor or business executive—or perhaps climbed to even greater heights. Instead, shortly after high school, and still in her teens, she married. She and her hus-band decided to have a large family together, which she dedicated herself to raising.

In everything she had done before in life, Sara had brought her many natural talents to bear, and she now applied those gifts for the benefit of her own young family. When her children had an essay to write for school, she would tutor them through it, focusing not only on grammar and wording but also on the logic and presentation of ideas, and on how to make academic concepts come alive. She seemed at her best when coaching others to be in charge. When one of the other neighborhood children was having trouble in school, she would invite them over to her house and have them turned around in no time; she'd get them reading, get them writing, and get them wanting to achieve on their own. She was very, very clever about motivation and about understanding how people learn, and taught in a way that increased other people's confidence in their own abilities. (I've spent my career in academia and had the privilege of seeing some extraordinary educators in action—and Sara ranked with the best of them.)

Despite the demands on her with eight children of her own and a family that was by no means wealthy, she continued to give to others. She took in a local foster child, and housed a young cousin from rural South Dakota to give her access to better schools than were available near her own home.

Then, when she was not yet forty years old, Sara's husband died of his first and only heart attack. With five children still left at home, she faced the daunting challenge of providing for the family single-handedly. Out of the workplace since high school, she had limited professional experience—and earning power. Yet given her independent streak and fierce pride, she saw providing for the family herself as the only option. At the same time, she knew that her children needed her time and her attention. She therefore chose a job based not on what was best for herself, but on what was best for them. This woman of enormous intellect and talent took a job as a janitor.

At the local municipal building and church, she earned her family's living by mopping up the floors and taking out trash. To supplement her earnings and allow her what would now be called "flex-time," she added to her regular daytime schedule with additional work from her children a few evenings per week and on Saturdays. The job provided only a slender income—but she was able to be home with her children every day when they left for school, and home for them when they returned.

I was one of those children.

For eight years, from the time I entered adolescence until I graduated from high school, I worked alongside my mother and my siblings, doing custodial work. I wish I could say that during those years I felt proud of my mother, of her adaptability and courage—particularly at a time when she faced her own sorrow at my father's loss—but I did not. Instead, I felt ashamed, believing that my mother's occupation was demeaning to her, and particularly embarrassing to me. It was humiliating to accompany her to the county sheriff's office and have people from our community come by and see us cleaning the place, sweeping floors or scrubbing up after some drunk. It was not with a joyful heart that I helped my mother with the grueling work that kept our family afloat. Yet when I grumbled or seemed resentful, she responded in a way that was simple and matter-of fact: We *have* to do this work, she would say—this is what we do, and this is how we live.

Only many years after graduating from high school did I realize that it was only my own thoughts and behaviors that were shameful. I had been re-sentful of what *I* had to do, yet my mother was the one with the enormous reservoir of untapped tal-ents—and dreams—who could have had an exciting career to which the world would have assigned more value. Where once I was ashamed of my mother the janitor, today I see her as what she really was, a hard-working woman who sacrificed enormously for me.

YOU WILL WALK a different path than Sara did. But what lessons might you learn from hearing her story?

Throughout your own life, you have been aided by many individuals. Some of the people who helped you did so at a cost to themselves, sacrificing their own dreams, aspirations, or pride. They may not have had to wash windows and scour toilets, but their work was hard, their sacrifices real—and by no means unique.

In any company you one day work in or lead, there will be janitors and managers, receptionists and executives, who through their efforts enable your company, and *you* as an individual, to thrive and be productive. You can be certain that those people, whose names you may not even know, are working hard for their own sake and for the company. But they are striving and sacrificing for their families at home, too.

When you begin to think about that company reorganization, and about the layoffs you might make, remember Sara's story. Realize that the employees whose lives you affect are all real people; *they are not numbers*. Each one is someone's son or daughter, father or mother. Each one is sweating and sacrificing so that others may thrive. Show them the same respect and consideration that you show to the people who sacrificed to help you.

Each one might be a Sara, someone who has made all the difference in another person's life—and who made the same in my own.

In the Moment

Frances X. Frei

FRANCES FREI holds an undergraduate degree in math, a master's degree in industrial engineering, and a Ph.D. in operations and information management, the latter from the Wharton School of Business. As an academic, she studies the drivers of customer satisfaction, operating efficiency, and company profit within services firms —from multibillion-dollar financial services conglomerates to luxury lodging concerns. She has created a second-year elective course, Managing Service Operations, and published in journals such as the *Harvard Business Review* and *Management Science*.

Students appreciate her toughness and clarity in the classroom as well as her accessibility out of it. Speaking in a blunt, confident manner, she punctuates her comments with easy laughter and her trademark emphatic pause.

I F YOU TOLD any of my undergraduate professors that I ended up being an academic myself, their first reaction would be *"Who?"* Their second would be total disbelief. During college, and even through grad school, I never imagined myself teaching. People who want to be teachers are usually the types who just *love* school, sit in the front row every day, and make Phi Beta Kappa. I was none of that. I never took academics seriously, ever. I never saw myself as a student. That wasn't my identity.

I was a basketball player. I majored in math, sure, but I was much better and more motivated on the court than in the classroom. To me, math courses were just complete, unimaginable boringness: The professor read verbatim from a sheet of notes and copied it onto the blackboard, and then we wrote everything down. That's *all* my classes ever were. I would sit there thinking, *Could you just make us a Xerox?* Because I saw very little reason to go to class, I rarely did. There were professors who wouldn't have been able to pick me out of a lineup, because they had never seen me. (If they had, they would have seen someone completely unexceptional, who sat at the back and slouched.)

While I was totally uninspired by academics, I loved sports. Basketball consumed my time and my thoughts. The team practiced every day: I went through hours of drills and practice shots, running and lifting weights. On alternate weekends we traveled to other campuses to compete—and when we played at home, I was supposed to think about getting to bed early and eating right so I would be fresh for the game. I was constantly surrounded by people who knew me primarily as a good basketball player. So that's how I became identified, as an athlete. That's how I was known to everyone else, and how I was known to myself.

After graduating from college I took a job for a little while, and hated it. About five minutes after starting I realized, *Whoa—this stinks.* While I had never liked school, I liked working even less. So, still completely turned off by academia, I went back to kill some time and avoid the professional world for a few more years. It didn't bother me at all that what I was studying—operations and information management—had no connection to what I had decided to do, which was to be a basketball coach. Dr. Tom Davis was my model. He was the men's coach at Iowa, and sportscasters always called him "Dr. Tom."

I was going to be Dr. Frances, the women's coach with a Ph.D.

And then it happened. Playing in an intramural league game, I blew out my knee. Physically, it was terrible; I needed three separate surgeries. Emotionally, it was worse. I could never be a serious athlete again, and I kept thinking, *What the hell am I going to do now?* It was a strange reaction, because I hadn't planned on *playing* basketball, but on coaching, which I certainly could have done with a bum knee. But the loss was deeper and more personal than that. For years I had staked my whole identity on something that had crumbled in a moment, and I felt like I had nothing left.

During the time I was having the surgeries, I found myself in real crisis. I had to alter how I saw my future, but I also started thinking about the past, and how I had approached basketball. I didn't really have regrets about my performance, because I had been in good shape, and played well. But I had never *appreciated* that time—I hadn't savored it. And because I never understood my ability to play as finite, I didn't do all those things you normally do when you realize an experience is fleeting. For example, I was in touch with *none* of the other players from my college team, because I never bothered to try and get to know them when we weren't on the court. I found myself wishing that somebody had done me a favor, taken me aside and, in whatever language I could have understood it at the time, said: *These moments are perishable. You only get eighty games, and each one of them, each minute, each shot, will be etched in your mind forever, but you can never have them back. Don't take this for granted.*

Because no one had ever said this, and because I was so confused, I was ready to take direction from anything, and for it to have deep impact: I was ripe to be imprinted on. And shortly afterwards, two important things happened. First, I was assigned a new academic adviser, a man completely different from anybody I had encountered in academia. Pat was generous, curious, and enthusiastic — not only about his own research, but also about his students' work. I still didn't like school, but I thought, *This man is my hero. I want to be like him!*

And second, I got to teach. Once. I was asked to run a review session for a tough, technical, graduate operations course. Many students in the class were foundering. Beforehand, I remember thinking, *No one is going to show up, and if they do, they'll never stay.* What could I, who was *so* unexcited about school, possibly offer a roomful of uncomprehending grad students? I had absolutely no idea. But when I set foot in the front of that classroom, everything changed.

Completely unbeknownst to me, I had a knack for understanding exactly what others *weren't* understanding—for seeing precisely where they had lost the thread of the material and gotten confused. (Later I realized that one of the core challenges of teaching was just that: being able to see stuff that comes naturally to you through the eyes of someone who struggles with it and finds it nonintuitive.) When I saw that the group of students had hit a speed bump, I somehow knew how to go down the road and meet them where the trouble was, and then how to help them get past it. I could just accompany them the rest of the way to comprehension.

Suddenly, I had a feeling of incredible leverage. I had found what I started referring to as a Fifteen Minute Opportunity: I could do more for that group of one hundred people in a quarter of an hour than I could achieve in *days* doing anything else.

That's when I knew I was going to teach. And I've been teaching ever since.

I CAME TO BE a professor by accident, in two different senses of the word. A real, physical mishap took away what I thought I was going to do with my life, and then a chance event—running a review session— pointed me toward what I was actually meant to do. After teaching that one class, things snowballed. I got good feedback from students, taught more courses, finished my Ph.D., took an academic job at another university, and a few years later got hired at Harvard. (Harvard, incidentally, had rejected me for college, graduate school, and first-year professorship. When I was offered a job here—let's just say I called my parents and bought the T-shirt.)

While I may have found this career by accident, the process itself was anything but painless; I still think of those years of playing basketball, which I never really appreciated. Ultimately those accidents affected not only what I do, but the manner in which I do it.

Today as a professor I want my students to understand what I didn't when I was playing sports, to recognize the *perishability* of their experiences here, to appreciate them in real time—but without having to go through the knee surgery or the identity crisis to get there. I want them to savor their own fleeting experiences, particularly here, in a place that offers such high expectations for them both as students and as leaders. This whole experience only lasts two years—they get only so many classes, so many chances to learn and achieve, and then it's over. So I help my students out. I make the high expectations this school offers palpable, and I make them clear. I run my classroom in such a way that students in it *have* to live up to the standards that this institution and their peers have for them. I make it so they can't waste time, or take class for granted: They have to be fully contributing, fully engaged—they have to be in the moment.

Now, when students walk into class, they're not always *aware* of the exact nature of the opportunity they're facing. There are eighty-five other people in the room, all of whom are smart and hardworking, who contribute ideas to help drive the group's learning process, and are civil to each other on the way. So the bar is set high—but only for a short while. Because no matter how hard any one student tries tomorrow, he or she can *never* have this experience again. This class has a shelf-life of exactly eighty minutes, and when that time is up, that learning experience, that discussion, that time with their peers, is gone—forever. But people don't always understand that, and sometimes they get a little lazy.

When students come in here a little tired, or uncaring, and thinking it's OK to bring anything less than their A-game, I step right in with a reminder of where they are and what they need to do. If they saunter in late, have nothing to say when I call on them, or start to zone out—I bring that to their attention, fast. Recently, for example, a guy came into class with his breakfast, and as we proceeded with the case study he sat there nonchalantly sipping his coffee and eating his bagel, gazing around the room.

Between bites he slumped forward with his head on his hand, and periodically whispered comments to the woman next to him.

Now, in many environments, his behavior would be fine—but not in this one. Here the goal is not only to participate yourself, but also to learn from the participation of others, and therefore every single student needs to be focused on whoever else is speaking. And I'm sure there were more *subtle* ways of handling the situation than the one I chose. As class debate continued, I walked up to the back of the room where this guy was sitting and gently straightened his chair back into the fully upright and attentive position. In doing so, I reminded him that he was part of a conversation, one in which he shouldn't abdicate his responsibility of being an active participant. By taking away the obstacles between him and a 100 percent effort, I sent him back into play. It's a game he and his peers can only be in once, and I want to make sure that mentally, emotionally, and in every other way, they're in it *now*. I'm simply doing for my students what I wish someone had done for me.

Of course, students don't always *appreciate* my efforts. Recently one of them told me that she had been talking with a friend about their courses, and when she mentioned that she was in my class, her friend said: "I hear Professor Frei's a real hard-ass." I was just *stunned*. I couldn't believe that somebody had actually said that about me, much less repeated it to my face. "So what did you *say*?" I asked. "Well," my student said, "I told her, 'Yeah, I guess she is.'"

That comment took me aback, not because I have a thin skin—which I don't—but because how those students see me is utterly at odds with how I see myself, the way I do my job, and what I'm trying to provide. Now, I admit I have a way of telling the truth straight up when other people might sugarcoat it, and I know other students who think I'm tough (one of them even has a son who calls me "the strict professor," and the kid's only five years old). But my God, a "hard-ass"? No way. The way I see it, whenever I'm in class, I am *nothing* but generous. I'm helping people to not make the same mistake I did: taking for granted a part of their life that's unique, that's precious, and that's finite.

IN MANY WAYS, the classroom is no different from any other situation you're going to find yourself in as a manager. Whether you're playing on a team, leading a project, raising a family, or starting a company, your environment and the people in it will have high expectations for the quality of your work, for your behavior, and for *you* as a person. And, of course, I would urge you to try and live up to those hopes—metaphorically speaking, to come prepared to class, and to sit forward in your seat. I also urge you to see those expectations for what they are: a privilege. It's an *honor* to be held up to elevated standards, and to be given the chance to lead. Value and appreciate each chance you have to reach up to those expectations.

But I suggest that you go even one step further.

Find your *own* Fifteen Minute Opportunity, your own point of high leverage—whether it be in teaching or in writing, in organizing or in managing, in coaching or in listening. Use that as a tool to pass on the high expectations—to pass on the privilege—that you yourself have been granted as a leader. Give other people the *gift* of high expectations—inspire them to reach and achieve, make them strive, and let them demonstrate to themselves what they are capable of. Because in doing so, you will help people understand the idea of perishability, the importance of cherishing every basketball shot, every class, every project, every chance they have to excel and lead others.

Let them *be* in the moment.

Why People Will Work for You

Timothy Butler

TIMOTHY BUTLER is Harvard Business School's director of career development programs as well as the co-founder of Peregrine Partners, a career-assessment and executive-development firm. With a Ph.D. in clinical psychology, he has nearly twenty years' experience working not only with business school students and alumni, but also with private clients and corporations.

His research focuses on how to achieve individual satisfaction and success in business careers, and he is the author, along with Jim Waldroop, of *Discovering Your Career in Business*. Using sample data from thousands of interviewees, the two have developed methods for professional self-evaluation that provide specific, practical data for career planning and selection.

While serious and calm, his excitement and conviction come to the fore when describing his own work. This enthusiasm seems fitting in a man whose career has been dedicated to helping others find jobs they love.

D IANA'S SHOULDERS SAGGED. Sitting in my office, she said she felt lost, adrift—uncertain that the job she had loved was really for her after all.

She had been hired by a prominent consumer-products company to market a brand considered a household name, and she had spent her first weeks on the job poring over sales data to prepare her annual business plan for the product—which, she noted, was poorly publicized to certain customer groups. Would it be possible to position it differently, she wondered, and appeal to a broader set of buyers? A door had opened; beyond it, Diana guessed, lay higher sales.

She began the laborious process of evaluating her idea, crunching numbers, scanning customer data, and researching competitors. With all the analysis supporting her hunch, she spent endless nights at the office crafting new means of putting across the brand image in the media. Despite the grueling

hours, Diana found herself becoming ever more energized, spurred on by the promise of her work. During those few short weeks, she had never felt so fully
engaged professionally, so motivated by sheer excitement and a sense of possibility.

When she walked into her boss's office for the review meeting, the report was sitting on his desk in a
manila folder. Composed, he leaned back in his
chair and waited for her to sit before speaking.

Clearly, he said, she had worked very hard on the
document—but she was *completely* out of line. This
product was a longtime top seller, not by any accident. Didn't she realize that the new promotional
scheme could create real risk for the company? Her
job was to stay abreast of market research, he told
her, to look after details of the existing plan, and,
above all, not to move the helm one inch on a ship
that had been sailing in the right direction for more
than twenty years.

The boss's rebuke left her completely deflated.
Within weeks—and after she had come to me for
career counseling—Diana left her job.

What did the company lose when she quit? No
one will ever know. The firm itself, no doubt, never
even asked the question. But as she told me her story
and I witnessed all of her raw energy, her marvelous

and particular gift for developing and growing a business, it seemed clear that her employer had missed a gaping opportunity.

I AM A PSYCHOLOGIST and career counselor. In the past two decades I've consulted with thousands of people. Many find themselves in jobs poorly suited to their innate interests. Lured by the siren songs of money, prestige, or family opinion, they've landed in the wrong careers, and ask me for help getting back on course. Others, like Diana, come for a different reason: They've chosen the right industry, company, and department—each is a strong fit. But the fourth, and most critical, layer of job satisfaction—the boss himself, and his attitudes toward power, risk taking, and meaningful delegation—is a poor match. Without a sense of authorship of their own work, my clients like Diana have lost their previous passion for the job.

Today as an employee, you likely identify with Diana. But now I want you as a leader, current or aspiring, to consider the other side of the coin. Imagine yourself as her manager. Would you want Diana's talents for *your* business? How would you get them, and how would you make sure that they were fully realized? How would you encourage the connection Diana felt to her work, and let her keep her fire? To answer these questions, you must be willing to make a radical move: to place the career development of your subordinates at the forefront of your agenda as a leader.

As a manager you will be held responsible for making an organization productive. The power you have will be real and indisputable: By hiring and firing, your decisions will affect the financial security of the people who work for you and their families. As in all situations in which there is a power differential, you may rely on a potent source of human motivation to get work done—fear. However veiled, whether it is the direct threat of job loss or the specter of shaming in a public meeting, fear will get your subordinates to do what you want. I know managers at every level, in all types of organizations, who rely on intimidation as the primary instrument in their management toolkits, though few label it honestly.

The relationship between fear and control is important in understanding the attempt to motivate. Control requires that a less powerful person change his or her behavior to conform to the intentions of the more powerful, and is often exercised in a subtle, even polite, fashion. We can use the term in a complimentary or pejorative sense—"he's got the situation under control," or "he is a control freak." Always accompanied by the threat of sanction, control uses fear as its handmaiden, prohibiting diversity of vision or will.

But let me ask you what you *really* believe about human motivation. Do fear and control get people to perform at their best? Do you think people work well because they fear getting a bad grade, not having the answer when called on, being ranked lower than a colleague, or letting down a parentlike authority figure? Is shame the greatest motivator?

Or does exceptional effort come from *desire*? Does better work get done when people are excited about what they are doing, when the task before them touches on some barely definable energy waiting to be expressed? Do they bring their full selves to their jobs when they see that there is something to *create* at the workplace? Is something vital lost when creative insight and enthusiastic energy go uncultivated?

Please, do not answer too quickly. The issue is complex, and I have had highly regarded managers provide compelling evidence for the power of fear and shame. They point to businesses where lack of a firm hand from management has led to inefficiencies, not to mention the squandering of resources and market opportunities when an employee, given free rein, has made costly mistakes.

TO BECOME A LEADER who harnesses the full talents of the people who report to you, though, I would suggest you *must* give up control, sacrifice some measure of your own power, and relinquish fear as a management tool. If a subordinate like Diana has a vision that is to become available, to be realized, you must cede your control over her work. She has her style of getting things done, her style of communicating, her style of talking with business partners and customers. She has her way of managing those reporting to her, and her way of spending company money. True delegation lies not in having someone execute *your* ideas, but in allowing *someone else's* ideas to become real—to do business in the way that their vision dictates.

Empowered, that person begins to make a new reality out of a job situation. She now comes to *own* her professional output, to see it as something that she is *making*—an extension of her own self in her day-to-day activity. This begets more initiative: a sense that she is enlarging her presence in the workplace and investing as much of her energy as possible to create a bigger field of action. That field changes and expands your business, because you have ceded control and the work is being driven not by your subordinate's fear, but by her positive vision.

Paradoxically, as you relinquish fear as a tool, you yourself may be afraid of the consequences. Those consequences may seem too high a price to risk, especially in successful, established organizations, where the rule is "make no messes." How do you know that things will move in a good direction? Perhaps the employees lack talent or judgment. Perhaps they overestimate their abilities or motivation. Perhaps they do not have a vision, or the commitment to go the distance. What if they get it wrong? You'll have to answer to your boss—who perhaps is right after all. Diana's manager had been in the business a long time and was no doubt a savvy businessman and wise shepherd of company resources. His attitude, resistance to suggestion, and exercise of control may have been in the best interests of the company and its ongoing profitability.

COULD YOU trust Diana, or someone like her? How do you know?

Ceding control, delegating, and allowing another career to develop is really about *diversity*: about letting yourself truly experience another point of view. We often think of the word *diversity* in terms of differences of race, religion, gender, nationality, or sexual orientation. But I am talking about another meaning: the radical diversity of grasping the worldview of a person who sees and experiences things differently than you do. Honoring this diversity means suspending control, allowing another self to take a small (or larger) part of the business in the direction that it wills.

Yet for this diversity to flourish and benefit the organization, you must also confront one of the great challenges of the leader, a challenge that is essentially intuitive rather than analytic. You need to truly *understand* people, developing empathic relationships with your employees. Not empathic in a sense of gratuitous care-taking, but in the root meaning of the word—the ability to "feel inside." You need to have a sense of what each worker's unique energies are and to perceive where they can make a contribution that will in turn spark an even greater commitment. Excellent managers truly *see* their employees—they know them well and can find the challenges that will tap their resourcefulness and channel their excitement to help the organization, at the same time feeding the employee's growing sense of self. This represents a radical sense of career development.

Many have seen this issue differently. Karl Marx held that capitalism is fundamentally alienating, separating employees from a sense of work that is truly personal, that engages an individual worker deeply. Marx felt that because it is a contradiction for managers (as the minions of the "owners of the means of production") to relinquish control, capitalism and the authentic professional growth of employees are inherently antithetical. Is he right? The only answer that can be given is the one offered by people as they actually *experience* their lives within the organizations where they work.

I believe that managers can build highly productive organizations that recognize the personal enthusiasms of individual employees. I also believe that there really is a way to excise the darkness that Marx saw without simply finding kinder and gentler masks for ever more subtle methods of control and fear-based motivation.

Can you take on this challenge? First decide what you actually think. With the will to give up some of your own power and to delegate to others, and the core skill of deep empathy, you will allow the people you work with to find meaning and passion in their careers.

You will make them *want* to work for you.

The Mount Rushmore Question

Thomas J. DeLong

THOMAS DELONG earned his bachelor's and master's degrees from Brigham Young University and his Ph.D. in industrial supervision from Purdue. A professor in the organizational behavior unit, he studies the management of human capital, particularly within professional-services firms.

Before coming to Harvard Business School, DeLong served as managing director and chief development officer at Morgan Stanley, where he was responsible for the firm's organization strategy around people, globalization, and change. In addition to his work on the Harvard campus, he teaches in executive education programs around the globe.

Pensive, calm, and direct, he offers unusual insights into the management and development of people.

⚜ ⚜ ⚜

T HE SUMMER my daughter Catharine was eleven, she wanted me to take her on the motorcycle to Mount Rushmore.

I hesitated. Our family was living in Utah at the time, and I knew it would be a long trip, particularly for a child so young: an eighteen-hundred-mile stretch across Wyoming to South Dakota and back again. I would have to leave work behind completely for several days—never an easy task. Building a career in university administration, I was busy managing a department, doing research, and teaching, and it could be an all-consuming job. As a professor you never feel *finished*: There is always another chapter to write and course to develop. Yet my daughter was persistent. She had her heart set on seeing the monument, and she convinced me that she had the endurance to make the journey.

Part of my reason for taking Catharine on the trip was to broaden her horizons, to expose her to different people and experiences in a controlled way, with her father by her side. The time we spent in South

Dakota overlapped with the Sturgis Motorcycle Rally. Every year, one town over from Mount Rushmore, literally hundreds of thousands of bikers get together for their annual convention, the largest in the world. You can see *everything*: old grannies on bikes, whole families in matching black leather outfits, grizzled men who've been riding for decades. They all converge on Sturgis, which is a small town, to celebrate what they love to do. For a week, the activity never stops. In about two dozen tents set up out in a field nearby, people gather twenty-four hours a day to get tattoos.

Throughout the trip, Catharine was inquisitive, peppering me with questions about these startling new sights. But it was at Mount Rushmore itself that *she* startled me. We stood at the monument's base in a small crowd of other tourists, gazing up at the enormous sculptures of Washington, Jefferson, Roosevelt, and Lincoln.

"Dad, how were those leaders chosen?" Catharine asked.

They were courageous, I answered confidently. They had taken risks, tried to help others, and most important, they had made a difference in people's lives.

"Do *you* make a difference?" she queried.

Catharine's simple question surprised me, and no certain, easy answer came. *Was* I making a difference in other people's lives? How, in what ways? On the long ride home, past the craggy mountains and dense forests of Yellowstone and of the Grand Tetons, I pondered that exchange with my daughter.

CATHARINE'S QUESTION changed the nature of the trip, and in some measure, my life. It forced me to define exactly what kind of difference I sought to make, and how I sought to make it.

I decided that I wanted to create opportunities for the people in my life to take risks, to try new behaviors, to positively affect other people and organizations—and through my everyday behavior, I wanted to enable them to make the changes in their own lives necessary to seize these opportunities. In my daily interactions, in the way I spoke and acted, in how I made them feel about themselves, I wanted to help the people around me to grow, to become more self-confident and better able to get where they wanted to go.

YET ONCE I REALIZED how I wanted to affect other people, I had to figure out what actions to take, and in what ways to prepare myself to take them. I needed to ask myself two more difficult questions. Since then I've posed these same two questions to students, managers, and senior executives who want to use their time and talents to have a positive impact on others. (Students tend to stare at me when I ask them; executives begin moving around uncomfortably in their chairs.)

The first question is: How do people experience you?

The second question, which is more complex, is: How do people experience themselves when they are with you?

Understand that the important thing is not what you *say* to other people at a particular time, but what transpires *inside* those people when you are talking to them. What are they thinking and feeling? In what way, however small, has their perception of themselves changed as a result of having the interaction?

Take a specific example: Think of a typical interaction with one person in your life, something short and routine—say that on the way to work, mind racing about what you want to achieve in the office, on your big presentation to senior management, you stop for a cup of coffee. You grab the paper cup from the woman behind the counter (the same one you see every morning), hand her the money, and leave, all the while mentally jotting a list of to-dos.

Imagine how the woman serving coffee experienced you. Did you seem friendly, say thank you, smile? Or did you wordlessly grab the cup, not making eye contact? How do you think she experienced *herself* in that brief encounter—as appreciated, or invisible?

The opportunities to influence individuals in a positive way permeate every aspect of our lives, from home to work. At the office, when a junior employee works back-to-back late days to finish a special project and then asks you for feedback, does he walk away from the conversation feeling competent, capable, and energized—that he has learned from your expertise—or disheartened by the disinterest you have shown him? When you get home from work, tired at the end of a long day, how does your spouse perceive you, perceive herself? Are your first words when you walk through the door ones which make her feel loved, appreciated, and central to your life—or does your abruptness make her feel deflated?

How have you made a difference in those other lives?

AS LEADERS we have a dynamic power to better the lives we touch, to help people gain more positive perspectives on themselves. But we can't achieve this casually, by just quickly running through this list of questions. Our approach has to be serious, and systematic.

Start a spreadsheet: List all the people in your life. Include family members, coworkers, friends—

cast the net wide. Using that list, keep track for one month of how much time you spend interacting with each person on it, and what type of interactions they are.

Watch for the patterns that emerge. You routinely ignore a friend until he has called you three times, and eat lunch at work every day with the same small group of coworkers. You are usually curt to your office's receptionist, or spend most family dinners mentally absent, wondering if some important e-mail from the office has arrived.

I've developed this method over the years since my trip with Catharine, and applied it in a variety of circumstances. In that time, I worked as the chief development officer of Morgan Stanley, setting strategies for human resources. I once asked a very senior managing director, the head of a large department, to try this exercise.

Four weeks later he came back to me with his daily diary, stunned. He spent most of his work time, he realized, dealing with 20 percent of his staff—lavishing praise on the superstars and trying to boost the performance of the weakest. The middle band, 80 percent of his reports, the dozens of people who made the department run by coming in every day and often staying at work all night, completely dedicated to doing their jobs, were ignored. In an effort to create an excellent department, he had inadvertently sent them the message that they were unimportant, unworthy of his attention.

Once this exercise allowed him to see the problem, he was able to start correcting it. Changing the way he worked, he divvied up his time more evenly among all the people who reported to him. He tried to praise and motivate, to encourage his employees to reach higher, for goals they had not thought achievable. He saw himself beginning to make a small difference where before he had not even thought to direct his energies.

TO START focusing intently—and with some degree of effort—on how you affect others is much harder than you think. It goes against the grain of who we are as high achievers, accustomed to accomplishing great things and pursuing our *own* successes. We consistently pass up the chance to touch the lives of others, to change them for the better, in the small, routine encounters that make up a day. We focus on areas of our lives in which it is easiest to demonstrate accomplishment, on awards, honors, degrees, salaries, and titles—signals that we can brag about and point to, that demonstrate that we continue to be successful people. Obsessed with our own goals and agendas, hungry for validation, we develop tunnel vision.

With each achievement our field of vision narrows, and all we can see is our own next victory. We get good grades one semester and immediately plan how to get on the dean's list the next; we earn our first yearly bonus and then wonder how much money next year will bring; we get promoted to vice president and then wonder when the corner office will be ours. Our habit of success becomes an addiction, and we always need more, constantly craving proof of our own worth.

But in doing so, we confuse individual professional accomplishment for leadership. Seeing only our careers and achievements, we miss the small opportunities for positive influence that occur constantly around us. It becomes increasingly hard to see opportunities to affect other people's lives, and to place those opportunities—whose rewards are often invisible—ahead of our own ambition. Leadership, though, is something different from ambition, or from simply achieving goals: It involves inspiring, motivating, and creating opportunities for others.

Redefine your success. You *can* be a leader without seeing your face writ large in stone, towering above. Begin to measure your achievement in how you affect others, in the difference you make in the people around you, in how you enable them to make changes in their own lives—not in how you burnish your own résumé. Resist your dependence on the milestones of success and embrace being a leader with a small "l."

I TOOK CATHARINE on the motorcycle expedition to open up her horizons. In the end, she was the one who affected me, stretching a short trip out into a lifelong journey.

BUILDING
VALUES

The Race

Henry B. Reiling

HANK REILING teaches in Harvard Business School's finance unit. He joined the school's faculty in 1976.

Professor Reiling's academic work has focused on the intersection of accounting, financial, and legal issues in management. This unique set of interests reflects his own multidisciplinary training, for in addition to an undergraduate degree from Northwestern University, he holds both an M.B.A. from Harvard and a J.D. from Columbia. His current research centers on the complex issues confronted by family businesses as their leadership transfers from one generation to the next. In addition to classes in finance and taxation, he teaches, and codesigned, the School's required course in ethical leadership and decision making.

With his signature turns of phrase and gentle Kentucky drawl, he leavens even the most dense course material, and the elective classes he teaches are among the School's most popular.

I HAVE A confession to make.

In the spirit of fairness and full disclosure, I must report that on multiple occasions over the years, Harvard Business School has performed studies designed to figure out which factors are correlated with a student's future achievement. We've looked at courses taken, marks earned, and all manner of other variables, including height. Unfortunately, there seems to be no relationship at all between the grades a person receives here, and his or her later degree of accomplishment. Short-term correlations, yes; long-term, none at all.

And this isn't just a business school phenomenon. The list of the past century's greatest leaders includes many who were at least occasionally low-wattage, academically. Future British Prime Minister Winston Churchill was a mediocre pupil at his British secondary school who twice failed Latin and therefore his college entrance exams; future President John F. Kennedy earned C's in his early years as an undergraduate at Harvard College. Alfred Sloan, the organizational genius who shaped General Motors into the twentieth century's most powerful company, made D's in the required humanities courses at the Massachusetts Institute of Technology. And although Franklin Delano Roosevelt later managed to pass the bar exam, he failed to graduate from Columbia Law.

There are two key points to take away from all of this. The first is that short-term academic wins and losses must be kept in perspective. Life takes many laps around the track, and the very top and the least successful students at a place like Harvard still have two-thirds of the race left. Front-runners—like the people who've earned straight A's—frequently fade over the long distance, while those previously at the back of the pack pick up their pace. The second point is that however far into the race you are at the moment (or five years from now, or fifteen) it is useful to have an idea as to what factors besides intelligence *do* produce success—and an understanding of how all those factors fit together.

This is a topic the academic world itself has wrestled with for decades. The most famous study on the subject began in 1921, when cognitive psychologist Louis Terman began tracking fifteen hundred children—or "Termites" as they came to be known—

each of whom had an IQ of 135 or higher. Because over time the Termites not only academically out-performed but also outearned the average American, the study pointed to inborn intelligence as a strong predictor of future achievement. However, an even more interesting insight came from several follow-on and satellite studies. The highest- and lowest-achieving Termites—and the gap between the two groups was significant—had nearly identical IQs. Those in the more successful bunch, however, all possessed two characteristics which set them apart: high degrees of confidence and of persistence—or a kind of "fire in the belly."

Now, as businesspeople, we believe that the de-tails of implementation are critical: we think about situations in terms of where the proverbial rubber meets the proverbial road. It would seem, therefore, that to study the true drivers of success, we need to go deeper than the academic answers of intelligence, confidence, and persistence.

There's an old saying that a smart person learns from experience, but a *really* smart person learns from *other* people's experience. And since I have a head start on you in years—and therefore in observing the experiences of other people, including the members of my own business school graduating class—I'd like to share a few impressions on what those other factors are, and how they work together.

While I am by no means an auto racing buff, it seems to me that what determines life success is similar to what makes a championship car at the Indianapolis 500, Monte Carlo Grand Prix, or on the NASCAR circuit. In any of those events, having the most powerful engine—the brain—doesn't mean you're going to win. You need precise steering, good brakes, firm suspension, a fuel tank big enough to get you where you're going, excellent judgment behind the wheel—and, as one of my students recently remarked, you need a great pit crew, too. No one or two or three *individual* elements—such as the ability to get high grades—can get you to the finish line first. With race cars as with life, it takes many well-integrated parts to really be successful. And in my opinion, among all those different parts, five not yet mentioned are critical.

FIRST IS THE ABILITY to handle disappointment. The highly successful people I mentioned above were all able to weather their academic disappointments, persevering through their academic "slick spots." You also must deal with disappointment in a wider sense—you must handle letdowns in *all* spheres of life. Throughout your career you're going to encounter some extremely frustrating, even painful, events. You may work in a company that's the target of a takeover, and suddenly there's no need for two vice presidents of finance, so you get let go.

The successful person simply goes on with life, meeting disappointment and hard knocks with resilience, like a sturdy old coffee mug at a roadside diner: drop it, and it just sort of *bounces*. It probably fell off the server's tray earlier in the day, and it's going to fall again later—and bounce again. Sometimes people who have experienced a lot of success early on in life—getting into the college of their choice, perhaps, or graduating Phi Beta Kappa—haven't developed their diner-mug characteristics; they don't know how to shake off failure or disappointment and keep on going. They're more like a lovely china teacup: exquisite, delicate, beautiful to look at— but fragile and apt to shatter when adversity strikes.

The second part is luck—and by luck I don't mean being born to wealth or position or winning the lottery, because my definition of luck is a little different from the traditional one. To me, if you've received good genes—which you have—had a decent education—which you've had—and had some mentors or people who cared about you and gave you some good advice, if you've got access to this country, and were born in this era and not in the Middle Ages—well, then you've already had more than your fair quota of luck. (And if you find a partner you truly respect and love who will put up with you for a long time, then you are *really* lucky.) Contrary to popular opinion, being lucky does *not* mean having an easy life. Ask the Queen of England or your favorite athlete if life is perfect for them, and they'll probably say no. Nobody is ever so privileged as to have everything in life go right, so luck can't be defined that way. Good luck is simply the absence of very *bad* luck: not getting hit by a truck while stepping off the curb, or having the same thing happen to a loved one. As already one of the most fortunate people on the planet being a lucky person just means getting to start off from a reasonably level playing field with your comparably lucky peers.

The third is the curious quality of "leadership." Because there are so many different types of good leaders, and they show up in so many different circumstances, good leadership is difficult to define; it's easier to think about leadership as what it *isn't*, rather than what it *is*. And what *doesn't* make for good leadership, as best as I can tell, is the singular drive to make money. Excellent leaders aren't economic animals; improving their own finances is well down their list of priorities. Napoleon once observed that men will "fight long and hard for a bit of colored ribbon"—The Legion of Honor—and he was right. Generals don't lead troops into battle thinking, *hot dog, I'm going to make another few hundred dollars today!* They do it for the honor or protection of their country. Likewise, any other great act is unlikely to be motivated by the prospect of higher pay. Mothers and fathers don't risk their lives for their children while pondering the value of their pension accounts; firefighters don't run into burning buildings and race up the stairs because they think they're going to profit. Great leaders are motivated by their concern for other people, or by causes greater than themselves.

The fourth part is a sense of fairness. You've got to be fair to other people, and I mean that not as a philosophical comment but as a practical one. To become successful you're going to need the best people working for you. If you treat those people in a way that's unfair or underhanded, and they have other options, as good people usually do—why, they'll leave. You'll have to get second-rate folks to take their spots—and it's going to be *awfully* hard to do well surrounded by second-rate people. If you want your organization's work to be of high quality, fairness and decency are required.

It's easy to list out these four determining factors of success, but it can be hard to imagine what the combination would look like in a living, breathing person. How might that person act, manage him or herself, and deal with difficult situations? Let me tell you a little story about the fifth factor: judgment.

A SHORT WHILE before graduation in 1993, one of our students was informed that he had achieved the honor of becoming a Baker Scholar, meaning that his grades had landed him in the top 5 percent of his class. The title of Baker Scholar carries with it great prestige; it stays on the résumé forever and opens many doors. With so many bright and industrious young people at the School, earning the honor is proof not only of a high natural intelligence, but also of an incredible work ethic. Nobody becomes a Baker Scholar accidentally.

No one, that is, except this young fellow. Each year, the exact grades needed to achieve that ranking shift slightly, and after he was notified by the registrar's office, this guy ran his numbers against the year's standard. They didn't compute. He ran them again—and still couldn't make it all add up. It dawned on him that there had been a mistake.

Now, most people in his shoes, the beneficiaries of an error like that, probably would have let the situation stand. They might have thought, *heck, it's their award. They're world-class experts in giving grades, and world-class experts in calculating grades, and if they're not good enough at math or they don't have enough computing power in the back office to figure this out, it's not my problem.* But not this guy. He called the registrar himself and pointed out what seemed to be an oversight. No fanfare, no fuss—and for him, no more Baker Scholar. The rest of the winners got to have dinner with their mamas and their papas and the School's deans; this guy got the lesser designation of "Honors" on his transcript and got to go to a separate event with the head of the M.B.A. program. That was about it—until the graduation ceremony itself. On Commencement Day, the dean of the school told this story to the graduates and assembled guests. When he finished, the class was immediately on its feet with an enormous and sustained round of applause.

Now, we can safely assume this guy had ample smarts, confidence, and fire in the belly. Drilling deeper, there's no question that he possessed the first four elements I've described. He must have been very disappointed, yet rose above his disappointment. His mere presence at graduate school tells us he had been lucky. Money could not have been his main motivator, for he gave up an enormous professional asset. He demonstrated a keen sense of fair play. Looking at all the guy had going for him, one couldn't help but be impressed. Without a doubt, a bright future awaited him.

But that's not why I or anyone else in that crowd was clapping. We were celebrating the soundness of his decision; in a tricky situation, he had had the instincts to go that extra mile and to do the right thing. He demonstrated personal standards and style that were well above the ordinary. His classmates were acknowledging the most important element of all, the one that takes control of the other four, and brings them all together: good judgment. We weren't applauding a well-built car with a powerful engine and sensitive brakes. We were applauding a winning *driver*—a person with the emotional maturity and good sense to make the right decisions under pressure. We saw someone we trusted—and admired— behind the wheel. Suppose he calls you looking for a job: it's likely you would try to help. If you found out we'd be working with him, you'd feel confident about having him as a colleague. If one day he managed any of your investment accounts, you wouldn't have anxiety about him cheating you. If trust and admiration were bankable assets, this man had just made a huge deposit.

AS YOUR PROFESSOR, I consider myself to have something of a vested interest in how you turn out:

I *want* you to be successful. You already have the intelligence, and I hope, the confidence (without being arrogant), and that fire in the belly. I also hope that throughout your career you will be tough, lucky, selfless, and fair.

May great success be yours—achieved with good judgment, and in the right way.

The Oath

Nitin Nohria

NITIN NOHRIA is both a professor of organizational be-
havior and director of research at Harvard Business
School. He holds a bachelor's degree from the Indian
Institute of Technology, Bombay, and a Ph.D. from
MIT's Sloan School of Management. He came to Har-
vard upon his graduation from Sloan in 1988.

Concentrating his work on personal leadership and
organizational change, he is a prolific author who has
written or cowritten ten books—among them, *Driven:
How Human Nature Shapes Our Choices* and *What
Really Works: The 4+2 Formula for Sustained Business
Success.*

Known to confront a single student with questions
for a quarter of an hour at a time, he is widely regarded
as one of the school's most demanding instructors. Yet
while the standards he keeps for his students are high, he
also communicates an unwavering—and energizing—
confidence that they will be met.

FROM AN EARLY AGE, I knew I wanted to be part of the institution of management. I wanted to spend my life deeply engaged in the positive engine of corporate enterprise. I wanted to learn what it takes to lead effectively. This was my father's legacy, and my most precious inheritance.

There was little in the beginning of my father's life to suggest that he would enter management, or even become a white-collar professional. He grew up in India, in a small village called Dharamkot, a few miles from the border with Pakistan. When he was ten years old, his own father died. My father spoke to me often about his early years, about the conditions he lived in, ones which today I would label poor, and even primitive: He walked miles each day to the nearest school and returned each evening to do his homework by the only available light, the flame of an oil lamp.

Given the circumstances of his boyhood, the most he could have realistically hoped for was to rise to become a local merchant, a small-time trader. My father, however, was a remarkable man, as ambitious as he was intelligent. Not only did he manage to complete his secondary education, but he also went on to university to study engineering. After his graduation, he landed a position at Phillips—and, when he was thirty years old, shortly before my birth, won a scholarship to study in England, at the Manchester Business School.

I suppose we all have very different types of relationships with our parents, and the one I had with my father was deeply intellectual. Throughout my childhood, starting when I was very young, he spoke to me candidly and in detail about his work. He described the challenges he faced as a manager, and how he sought to apply his skills to best overcome them.

I watched the thought and energy my father poured into his role as a business leader, his care and diligence, his conscientious efforts to hone his abilities and do his best in the workplace. I grew to appreciate the positive power of business management—and not only in its profound impact on my father's life and the life of my family. My father's company benefited not only us but also all its other employees, as well as the communities in which it operated, selling its products and services. It created tangible value for many.

My entire career has grown out of an early fascination with the value of leadership, with the complexities of human behavior, and with the demands of workplace performance. I've coached executives and taught graduate school, written books, and sat on the boards of companies. I've examined tough, real-life management problems in governmental, industrial, medical, and academic organizations. And with each of these problems my goal has been the same: to figure out how leaders can solve them.

While I've always worked for a university, and my paycheck comes from Harvard, I have never seen myself solely as a "professor" or "academic," with the distance or passivity those words might imply. I don't just *study* management; I'm not some neutral outside observer watching it passively through a one-way mirror—I'm *part* of it. Management is my calling; it is the thing to which I have proudly devoted my entire professional life.

But in 1991, the actions of a handful of executives threatened to tarnish my life's work. The economy had begun to slow down, and over the following year veered into recession. American business suddenly faced a crisis of great proportion; every day, newspaper headlines blared announcements of enormous losses at even the most prestigious corporations, ones that had previously embodied a kind of unassailable stability and strength. Corporate America was virtually awash in red ink.

And this recession was *different*. Not because it was fierce and persistent (for there have certainly been downturns of greater length and severity before), but because there was a feeling that large industry was at a cusp, a real crisis point—and because of a pervasive sense that senior management *itself* was involved in creating this crisis. Much of the media coverage focused on those massive company losses and on the rapidly swelling ranks of the unemployed. Yet it also centered on stories about outrageously high CEO pay, about how some top executives had taken the recession as a chance to pursue mergers and layoffs with an appalling zeal. The stereotype of the slash-and-burn manager was born, and figures such as "Chainsaw" Al Dunlap became sudden celebrities. Business leaders became widely perceived as capable of breaking every bond of trust with their employees and other stakeholders. If not actually to *blame* for the terrible economy, they appeared actively—even happily—complicit in meting out its ill effects.

This was an enormous shift in how management as an institution was seen. Previous business slowdowns had appeared external, as the function of uncontrollable events occurring on a macro scale, well beyond the control of any individual executive. War, inflation, the high price of oil—*these* were the drivers of recessions past, *these* were the factors which had prompted previous cinching of the corporate belt. Management itself wasn't the villain.

At the time, I had just been promoted to associate professor, one rank below tenure. It was a pivotal moment in my career: I needed to launch a large-scale research project that would let me demonstrate my mettle as an academic. And the events of that year provided an ideal subject for study.

Over the following few years, I got deeper into my research, observing dozens of these companies on the brink. And at the same time, forced to watch the gradual corrosion of public trust in business management, I grew increasingly angry. Those chainsaw-wielding businesspeople—they weren't just debasing their own reputations, they were devaluing the entire profession, and the work of its every practitioner! As I watched that taint creep over management, I was furious. I imagine other businesspeople were equally indignant. Yet as a group, we stayed curiously silent, not standing up in a public way to repudiate the actions of bad managers and reclaim the profession for ourselves. And now, again, ten years on, with so many other examples of management malfeasance, we face a similar fiasco—perhaps an even worse crisis of faith in business leadership.

I'VE ASKED MYSELF how to prevent further damage
to the profession, how to stop more managers from
making poor choices, and how to try to set the existing problem right. How can management construct
a collectively agreed-upon moral foundation? How
can its members stand up and defend our profession, restoring its legitimacy and good name? How
can we cultivate a sense of ownership of our field so
that it can become an asset so fundamentally valuable to all of us that nobody would risk letting it be
harmed?

I began to reflect on what set management apart
from its comparable disciplines, and to wonder how
they enjoyed better standing in the public's eye and
encouraged better behavior in their ranks. One
thing immediately struck me. Other professions
have standardized codes of conduct: Physicians take
the Hippocratic Oath; attorneys are sworn in to the
bar. These codes, I think, have enormous impact on
the way the professions are perceived — in suggesting
what they represent, and in thus creating a sense of
social value. There is a generally accepted vision of
the profession within our culture; we all know that
doctors "do no harm," that they work to cure the
sick. My eight-year-old daughter says she wants to be
a physician when she grows up, I think because she

grasps that doctors use their special skills to *help* people, and that the job is something to aspire to.

Like medicine, management requires expertise and skill, considerable training and apprenticeship, and it allows you to positively affect lives on a constant basis. Why then is becoming a doctor seen as being selfless and creating social value and becoming a successful businessperson seen as the reverse?

Business enterprises have, over time, contributed more to the good of society than any other endeavor. In terms of jobs created, families supported, economic development achieved, and scientific and technological breakthroughs reached, business has been unparalleled. Yet that isn't the typical public perception of management, nor of managers of themselves.

Why not, I wondered, create our own code of conduct? I don't mean something that lays out basic moral codes or repeats what is found in law—"thou shalt not steal from thy employees," and so on—but something motivating, that encourages respect, learning, and upstanding behavior? Something direct and clear, that managers could keep at their desks and refer to when we need guidance and inspiration? Why not have a statement of *mission* for managers as a group, which outlines our highest standards of skill and responsibility?

The current rash of corporate scandals is far from over, and its effects are acutely felt. But *this* time, I'm not going to stand by mute. With a set of guiding principles in place, we as a group can begin to fix what has been broken. We can give ourselves back the energy and hope we need—and earn back the credibility and trust we deserve.

The Management Oath

As a manager I am entrusted with one of the most important resources of my society: Enterprises that create great value for its inhabitants. In vowing to uphold that trust, I acknowledge my responsibilities as an agent of the public interest in well-managed enterprises, and therefore make the following promises, freely and upon my honor:

I will continually seek to enhance the value my enterprise creates, whether in the form of goods and services, jobs, or economic return, and to have that value be both genuine and lasting. In fulfilling this fundamental duty, I will try to balance the many, and sometimes divergent, interests of the constituencies that my enterprise serves.

I will uphold, both in letter and in spirit, the laws governing my own conduct and that of my enterprise, making my personal behavior consistent with the values I publicly espouse and remaining vigilant to the integrity of others. I will never allow the prospect of personal benefit to outweigh the interests of my enterprise.

I will represent information about my enterprise to all relevant parties in a manner that is timely, clear, and accurate. I will make decisions in a transparent manner so they do not appear subject to individual whim or idiosyncrasy, and will do my best to protect the interests of those who may have little power, such as the individual investor, temporary employee, or small customer.

I will make business judgments based on the best available knowledge, remaining unafraid to say "I do not know," but consulting colleagues and other resources outside my enterprise as needed. I will always retain the humility to reconsider my decisions and opinions in light of new evidence.

I will respect the skills and wisdom inherited from previous generations of managers, and offer what I have learned gladly to any person I may mentor or teach. I will do my part to be innovative and develop management as a profession, so that its contribution to the well-being of society may continue and grow.

Remember Who You Are

Kim B. Clark

KIM CLARK became dean of Harvard Business School in 1995. During his tenure, he has presided over significant enhancements to the school's technological platform, research efforts, and physical plant. Yet though certain aspects of the school have changed, its fundamental mission remains unswerving: *to educate leaders who make a difference in the world.*

Clark's roots in the university's community run deep, with his B.A., M.A., and Ph.D. degrees in economics, all from Harvard. A member of the business school faculty since 1978, he is himself a highly distinguished business scholar, a specialist in manufacturing management who has coauthored eight books.

More arresting than his credentials, however, is his unshakable belief in the importance of leadership education. He speaks in deliberate, even tones, fixing his audience with an intent gaze, conveying his conviction. Whether addressing first-year students or CEOs, they cannot help but listen.

⚜ ⚜ ⚜

M Y MOTHER PASSED AWAY in 1998; my father
two years ago this June. I loved both of my
parents very much and miss them terribly. But as
much as I feel their loss, I know they are with me
every day—in what they taught me and in the
advice they gave me. Their messages continue to
guide me today, and as you go forward in your
lives, I'd like to share them with you.

THE FIRST PIECE of advice comes from my mother.
My mom was an intense woman. Barely five feet
tall, what she lacked in stature she made up for in
dynamism. She had dark hair, sparkling eyes, and
endless energy that she lavished on her kids. She believed in and loved us so much, it *poured* out of her.
She was raised four blocks from Utah State University in a highly academic family: One of her brothers
became a college dean and the other a distinguished
doctor and professor of medicine. She had aspirations

for her children, and wanted us to set high standards for ourselves.

"Kim!" she would say every morning as I left the house, leaning her face down into mine and looking me straight in the eye. "You go out there today and be a leader. Stick to your guns about what you know to be right and wrong, and don't let anyone else drag you around by the nose. Remember who you are!" Every day my mother's message to me was: Remember all those people who worked and sacrificed to make it possible for you to be where you are. Remember that when you walk out this door you carry a mantle of responsibility, the good name of this family, the hopes and dreams of your mom and dad. Remember the promise that is yours, the wonderful opportunities in front of you, the hope that is in you for a better world.

It was a lot for a little kid in elementary school, early in the morning, lunch box in hand, to carry off to school every day. But it is such good advice. My mother insisted that I set high standards for myself— not only in what I did, but in how and why I did it. And she didn't just offer advice: She was vigilant about helping me live up to it.

While I was still in kindergarten she enrolled me in an elocution class. Twice a week for the next five years, she dropped me off at the studio of Mrs.

Grace Nixon Stewart. Mrs. Stewart was a theater director, acting coach, and voice teacher. She assigned us vocabulary words, short scenes or monologues, even Shakespearean sonnets to learn. We were expected to commit these fairly complicated passages to memory, and then required to perform the piece for the group on Saturdays.

Each morning, my mother got me up early to practice my assignment. She didn't go into another room while I rehearsed, but actually sat there in front of me to listen and coach. (Remember, I was five years old.) There were days where I was still half-asleep, the piece unmemorized and my performance groggy at best. "Kim," she would interrupt, "you're just putting in the minimum effort. If it's worth *doing*, it's worth doing *well*."

Besides a few passages (like Robert Burns's ballad "O my Love's like a red red rose/That's newly sprung in June…"), I've forgotten most of what Mrs. Grace Nixon Stewart had me memorize. The lessons my mother taught me, however, have stayed with me to this day. Part of that was due to sheer repetition: Throughout my childhood I heard those same exhortations all the time — and I mean literally all the time.

But more likely it was the meaning behind my mother's sayings. For what might have seemed like admonitions were actually affirmations of my mother's belief in me, and in what I was capable of. My twice-weekly elocution class was not just a means of polishing my public speaking, but a way of reinforcing my own faith in what I could accomplish. "Be a leader" didn't simply mean, Follow all the rules; it meant, Don't be swayed by the opinion of the other kids into doing something inconsistent with who you are, with what you know in your heart is right. Most important, when my mother said "Remember who you are" she meant: *I believe in you, and want you to live up to the promise that is yours, to the opportunities out there for you, and the hope that is in you to make a difference in the world.*

THE SECOND PIECE of advice comes from my father. My parents were opposites in many ways, dissimilar in both background and temperament. My dad was a wise and wonderful man. He was patient, gentle, and calm, a quiet leader. He was raised on a ranch near the bottom of Bryce Canyon, in an area that was—and still is—truly rural. He became the first person in his family to go to college.

When I was growing up, I knew my father as a typical dad in our typical suburban neighborhood in Spokane, Washington. He was an advertising manager for farming and ranching magazines, and he wore his thick, wavy hair slicked back—a very distinguished-looking man. But in his early life he had been a cowboy—a real one, who worked riding the range, herding cattle, and breaking horses. He knew what it was like to get up before dawn and do hard physical labor all day long.

That experience shaped him in multiple ways: He was always an extraordinarily dedicated worker, he had enormous reverence for education, and he loved to ride horses. He left the ranch to pursue his education and left that part of his life behind—but throughout his life, riding was his joy. His advice to me was a rich metaphor that came from that joy, from that love of riding, and it carries beautiful and profound advice. It is: *Ride the high country*.

My dad understood that we live our lives in the valley, focused on the day-to-day tasks in front of us, where things are more settled. But we do not always have to ride there. We can ride the high country where the light is intensely bright, where the sky is deep and blue, where it seems you can almost ride forever.

His message was: Set your sights high. Get up out of the valleys and the shadows of everyday life into the high country, where you can see forever. Soak up the light that is there and let your spirit soar, let the wind blow in your hair, let your heart dream big dreams, let your passion for life and for living and for making a difference run free.

WHILE MY PARENTS' messages were a familiar refrain throughout my childhood, it wasn't until the end of high school that I realized how they might guide me—in a concrete, real-life way.

As a senior in high school, I played in a rock band with friends in my class. We were dedicated, practiced constantly, and moved past the guys-in-a-garage phase and got to be pretty good. Suddenly we were getting paying gigs most weekends.

I was thrilled. Part of me was very wrapped up in that band. But another part of me was the oldest son in the Clark family, proud of my heritage, a faithful member of my church and a dedicated student busy applying to colleges. Without even telling my parents, I had applied to Harvard. No one in my family had ever gone there, and I didn't think I had much of a shot at getting in—but I wanted to try. So I was riding around being Mr. Cool Rock Musician half of the time, and the other half I was focused on family, church, and academic goals. I was running on parallel tracks.

When the group won a citywide Battle of the Bands, things heated up. My bandmates had stars in their eyes—we might be able to make it *big*. But I began to feel uncomfortable. I realized that I wasn't on parallel tracks, I was on *divergent* tracks: I actually was becoming two people, switching identities back and forth depending on who I was with. I had to make a choice.

As I considered my options, what I wanted to do and who I wanted to be, my parents' words were right there, helping to guide me. I remembered who I was, where I came from. I let myself dream about the future—and those dreams weren't about getting a record deal, letting my hair grow, and living in a tour bus. So I quit. My bandmates were shocked. They thought I was crazy to drop out on what they thought was the cusp of real success. But no matter how successful that band got, I knew it wasn't right. It wasn't in line with my aspirations, with my feelings of what I was meant to do, with who I was—it simply wasn't *me*.

In that instant and in many others throughout my life, my parents' advice has helped me recenter and refocus. I could remember who I was—the hopes and dreams I carried. And I could see the high country—where I wanted to go. At times my sense of what I should be building with my life has been vague, and my future has been unclear. But my mother and father's advice has been a critical part of my foundation.

TODAY, MY JOB is to help educate leaders of tomorrow — to develop their power to make a difference in the world. *That power exists in each and every one of you.* Each of you likely has your own foundation. It may not be the example of your parents that inspires you. It may be the advice of teachers, mentors, or friends. Or it may be your own principles, values, or faith. But I hope you will take my mother and father's words to heart. I hope that in whatever organization you work, no matter where you are, when those around you ask themselves, "Whom can we trust? In whom do we have confidence?" the answer will be you.

As you head off toward your future, I want you to know that enormous hope has been placed in you. The world ahead will be turbulent and uncertain: full of risk, and great reward. And within that world, business will be among the most dynamic forces. We need leaders who will make a difference in society, leaders who are firmly grounded in the highest standards of integrity and respect and personal accountability, leaders who are not afraid to set their sights high, who will dream and hope and believe in themselves and in those around them.

You are just the ones to provide that kind of leadership. So my counsel to you is very simple: Choose wisely and well. Find that anchor, that center of values and principles that should govern your life and stay true to it, hold onto it.

Remember who you are, and ride the high country.

About the Author

Daisy Wademan received her B.A. in history from Brown University in 1996 and her M.B.A. from Harvard in 2002. Before business school, she worked for four years in the investment banking and commercial lending divisions of J.P. Morgan & Co. Inc. She was born and raised in New York City, where she still lives. This is her first book.